It's never too late to start a scrapbook. Any time is the right time to begin a journal or make a beautiful frame for a special photo. Set aside time to create the legacy book with your family or friends or both (one weekend each month, one evening each week) and you'll soon find that it is time you anticipate with pleasure - time that yields rewards beyond measure.

Get started at a family reunion when you can talk with relatives, ask questions, and tape or video the answers as well as taking lots of photos and making notes. Looking at photos and mementos together will jump-start the process and provide so many priceless observations and facts.

Make sure that you include a title page in your album and a special page for who made the album, too. Start with a dozen pages. You can always add more.

Your legacy projects can have themes. An album can focus exclusively on holiday celebrations, birthday parties, the years spent in a particular home (lots of fun if you photographed it being built), the school years or religious events. An album can also be more inclusive and document events that happened that year, or if you fill an album more quickly it can span several months. Start a new one when the album is completely filled and won't hold more pages.

Make a mini-album each month or have several different albums in process at the same time.

Consider making duplicates if you have several children or siblings who would each like his or her own. A legacy album often doesn't include delicate original photos or documents so it's fine to use copies when you're making several of the same thing.

An Album filled with our Family Legacy

by Shannon Smith

The Hartman Family

In 1919, my Great Grandfather, Bernhard Hartmann, made the voyage to America from Germany. With him he brought his wife Trenfie and his three sons, Bernhard, William and Alfred, my grandfather.

My Uncle Bob was the first of four children to be born. He arrived four weeks early and at birth weighed only one pound. After spending a month in the hospital Uncle Bob was finally allowed to come home. Today he is 6'4" and weighs 220 pounds. Despite the fact that nobody thought he would live, he sure did grow up to be a big boy.

If our grandparents had known how much their pictures would someday mean to us I think they would have put them in an album with names and dates. Mine came to me in yellowed envelopes or in scattered albums with black pages and little writing. Sometimes there were a few faded pencil notes written on scraps of paper that offer scant information. I look at faces vaguely resembling my own and wonder who they are and where they were when a photographer captured the likeness. I've given up trying to find out whether that handsome couple lived to raise a large family or died young during a flu epidemic, though I admit I like to imagine happy endings and long lives. I didn't realize when we looked at them together in my childhood that so much would later slip my mind and that my grandparents would be gone. Like most children I thought that my loved ones would be around forever so I could ask questions whenever I wanted.

Some of us even rescue boxes of snapshots at a yard sale or when friends are sorting through late relatives' estates. I collect old photos because I love to make up stories to fit what I call my "adopted strangers."

PHOTO ALBUM

MATERIALS: *Books By Hand* materials in a pack: (two $1^1/4$" x 11" bookboards with three holes (the spine) A • two $8^1/4$" x 11" bookboards (front and back covers) B • Pages to go in between) • 2 pieces each of Legacy paper $7^1/2$" x 12" (front and back) C • 4 x 12" (front and back spine) D • $9^1/4$" x $10^1/2$" (covering for inside front and back) E • 72" of Ribbon • *Art Accents* Terrifically Tacky Tape

MAKE THE 'BOOKBLOCK' for the Album pages

On each page, with the embossed side facing up, fold over the space flap with two holes. Using a bone folder, press hard and crease each folded edge. To adhere the pages together, place tape along the spacer, without covering the holes. Stack the pages together, spacer side up, matching the holes and lining up the outside edges.

MAKE FRONT AND BACK COVERS

Mark a bookboard spine, piece A,. with an arrow pointing towards the long edge that the binding holes are closer to. This will be the hinge side of spine. Place spine paper wrong side down. Adhere the bookboard spine to the paper using tape. Make sure to leave $1/2$" margin on the top, bottom, and side edges opposite the arrow side of spine pieces. Clip the outside corners.

Measure $1/4$" away from the arrow side of the spine and lightly mark the distance with a pencil. Apply pink Tape along the line, and place bookboard cover B on paper, leaving a $1/4$" space between the spine and the cover. Apply Tape to the exposed paper edges and wrap them around the bookboard. To check placement, before applying adhesive, place Legacy paper, piece C, wrong side up and lay the bookboard cover on top. The paper should overlap the paper on the spine. Apply tape to the front side of the bookboard and place the bookboard onto the back side of piece C, leaving $1/2$" margin on the top, bottom and side. Clip the outside corners of the paper, apply tape to the exposed paper and wrap around the edges of the bookboard. Repeat the above steps for the second cover.

FINISH THE BINDING HOLES

Dab a very small amount of glue into each binding hole on the inside of the cover. Turn the piece over, and from the front of the cover, use a pencil point to punch holes through the paper. Make the holes as large as possible. This forces the paper to be glued to the inside of the binding holes.

MAKE THE HINGE

To check the fit, first center one of the end papers, piece E, on the inside cover. Then apply glue and lay, do not smooth, the paper onto the inside

Wouldn't it be wonderful *if people had always written journals and kept their pictures safe and documented? If you have inherited diaries or photos with names and dates, you're so lucky. And if the people who remember the "who, what, where and when" are still available, you're luckier still! Sit down with them soon and don't miss the chance to ask all your questions. As Giuseppe Mazzini wrote, "The Family is the Country of the Heart."*

Memory *isn't the only place where information should be stored, because memory is temporary and fragile, not always accurate. It may be too late to find out about the couple in my grandmother's photos, but I'm making sure that future generations will never have to guess when they see ours.*

A photo album to wear? *What a conversation piece! A beautiful frame? Yes, a single photo is a legacy, too! And what about making a new ornament each year for the tree or a refrigerator magnet you see every day? Not all legacy projects need to be albums and journals, not all of them need to include photographs... even miniature necklace albums give meaning to a precious memory.*

cover. Slowly bend the spine all the way back until it touches the outside cover. This will slide the end paper slightly away from the hinge edge of the cover. Place the cover end paper side up. With a bone folder, tuck the resulting paper "bump" into the hinge. Fold the hinge back a few more times to stretch the paper while it is wet with glue. Smooth the end paper down. Repeat the hole punching process. Repeat the above steps for the second cover.

BIND THE ALBUM

Place the inside of the back cover face up. Apply tape to the spine section, avoiding the holes, edges and hinge. Adhere the bookblock, with the spacers facing up, onto the back cover. Make sure the binding holes on the cover and the bookblock line up. Attach front cover in the same manner. Bind the album by keeping the ribbon tight. Using a pointed edge, push the end of the ribbon through the holes.

DECORATE OUTSIDE OF ALBUM

On the front cover, using the same ribbon, adhere to the seam of two Legacy papers. Place Gold filigree embellishments in the bottom corners and hot glue in place. Print book title on paper and using corner punches, make a mat frame around the outside and attach to the front of the album.

PAGES FOR ALBUM

MATERIALS: *Design Originals Legacy Papers* (#0478 Green linen, #0479 Green stripe, #0480 Green floral, #0484 Blue linen, #0485 Blue stripe, #0486 Blue floral, #0487 Rust linen, #0488 Rust stripe, #0489 Rust floral, #0494 Brown stripe, #0495 Brown floral, #0497 TeaDye letters, #0498 TeaDye tapestry, #0499 TeaDye music, #0500 TeaDye keys, #0501 TeaDye clocks)
• *Books By Hand* Ribbon Bound Photo Album • *Fiskars* scissors & paper trimmer • *Art Accents* Terrifically Tacky Tape • *Offray* Ribbon • *Printworks* Mulberry Paper • *Embellish It!*. Gold filigree embellishments • *Books By Hand* Paper glue • *Emagination* Corner punches • *Jesse James* Buttons and Decorative pieces • Hot glue gun • Craft knife • Bone folder
INSTRUCTIONS:

Cut paper to fit each page. Adhere to page. Cut a strip of coordinating paper, Vellum paper, a hand torn strip of paper, or a torn piece of mulberry paper. Attach to page. Place photos on the page with photo corners. Print or write journaling, layer and adhere to page with photo corners.

FAMILY

MATERIALS: *Design Originals Legacy Papers* (#0500 TeaDye keys, #0490 Coffee linen, #0493 Brown linen)
• *Creative Imaginations* eyelets • Deckle edge scissors • Gold Leaf pen
• Acid-free adhesive
INSTRUCTIONS: Cut strips of Brown linen paper and adhere to page. Cut photo mats from Brown linen and TeaDye keys papers. Adhere to page and embellish with flower eyelets. Write family names on photo mats.

Photographs as a Legacy

When photos are one of the legacies you have chosen to keep, picture someone looking at them a hundred years from now and try to answer the questions you know they would ask. Let your scrapbooks and albums bridge the years. Include the people who came before you and give pieces of your life to those who come next. Write down feelings and impressions in addition to names and dates.

Let young children tell stories and participate in making the pages. It's not just the older folks with stories to share. Your handwriting and spelling don't need to be perfect; your observations don't need to be profound. Include real life with all its celebrations and happy occasions and don't skip the rough times or losses, sadness and grieving. A legacy album can be especially precious when it records the life of someone whose years were few, as much as when it celebrates a very long one.

There is a saying "In family life, be completely present" (Tao Te Ching). I like to paraphrase it this way: In life, be completely present. Spend time right now making a scrapbook, frames, or mini books with your children and friends. The hours spent are part of the pleasure - you can even take pictures of the scrapbooking sessions (Mom and I Make Scrapbook Pages). Making something beautiful and creative with your pictures means your photographic legacy is a part of the past and the present, and for the future becomes a legacy ready to leave in other hands.

PARENTS

MATERIALS: *Design Originals Legacy Papers* (#0485 Blue stripe, #0486 Blue floral) • Cream Parchment paper
• *Embellish It!* Brass filigree embellishments
• Acid-free adhesive
INSTRUCTIONS: Use Blue striped paper as a background. • Cut a 5" x 11" piece of Blue floral paper.
• Print journaling from a computer on cream parchment paper and adhere to decorative papers.
• Embellish page with Brass filigree parts.

Each Legacy Comes in a Different Form

The word "legacy" is not defined by all people the same way and we don't all think of our legacies only in terms of photographs. Not every legacy is something tangible. Families grow, change, and take new shape, including step, adopted, and foster children. People without children have legacies to preserve and share, too. There are still family traditions, holidays and relatives. There are so many ways to define what matters, preserve what we've received and so many ways to create and leave legacies for future generations.

Photographs do top the list, but when it comes to tangible things, some of us would say that the legacy we received which matters most is a pocket watch, button jar and fabric scraps, or the family recipe box. Some of us would point to the bookshelf and call the family Bible and childhood storybooks cherished legacies. Others might show a lace collar or handmade quilt. My best friend would say it's her family's farm - what a legacy that land is. The memories I see in my father's black metal lunchbox are too numerous to count.

When it comes to intangible legacies, some would say the legacy they value most is the ability to sing, joke with family and tell stories, skills learned from family members or favorite teachers. Others would list patience or love of the water as a legacy. These are the legacies that have no shape or form till they're put into a journal and documented with pictures and objects - but they are legacies nonetheless.

A legacy is a place, a possession, something we've learned. A legacy is whatever we choose it to be. The intangible ones are the ones we can pass along by example, by teaching and by what we write. The tangible legacies are those things we create that can be handed to someone else like albums, frames, boxes, books, jewelry, and holiday ornaments - treasures that honor people, places and memories.

"Memory feeds imagination", shared author Amy Tan. Let this book be your starting point for preserving and creating meaningful legacies.

CHILDREN

MATERIALS: *Design Originals Legacy Papers* (#0493 Brown linen, #0494 Brown stripe)
• Cream parchment paper
• Gold filigree oval frame
• Gold corner mounts
• *7 gypsies* porcelain 'Journey' medallion
• *Offray* ribbon bows
• Acid-free adhesive
INSTRUCTIONS: Adhere papers, photos, frames, corner mounts and bows to scrapbook page.

Today's Thoughts and Yesterday's Remembrances...

Every memory is a precious legacy. The things you preserve for future generations become cherished possessions, but they are precious in the present as well. Sitting down with the family to look at a scrapbook page you made last week or last year is one of life's special pleasures. Sitting down with your grandchildren to look at those same pages many years from now makes it even more important that those pages be elegant and meaningful in color and design - treasures for their grandchildren someday, too.

Be a keeper of your legacy.
Safeguard and preserve the things you love for the people you love.

Maternal Family Tree

The Browne Family

Jenny McGill Schmidt

Ernest Schmidt

Nina Schmidt Reichl

Edna Fisher Martin

Raymond Reichl

Franklyn Reichl

Janet Reichl Browne

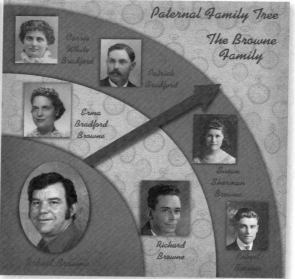

Paternal Family Tree

The Browne Family

Carrie White Bradford

Patrick Bradford

Erma Bradford Browne

Susan Sherman Browne

Richard Browne

Robert Browne

Robert Browne

FAMILY TREE 1

MATERIALS: *Design Originals Legacy Papers* (#0490 Coffee linen, #0501 TeaDye clocks)
• Dark Brown cardstock
• Acid-free adhesive
INSTRUCTIONS: With varying sizes of plates or a protractor, cut levels of family tree. • Glue on scrapbook page. • Journal names of family members. • Cut arrows and glue on page.

Your Family Tree
is an Important Legacy

Begin by gathering information for your family tree. Start by interviewing someone for more information on their life and the family. Instead of asking who, where, and when, you should be asking why, how and what.

The first interview should be short. Your goal is to gather the facts - names, approximate dates, places, stories about the origins of the family - so you can begin researching records. You should write all the questions out in advance that you are going to ask.

Be prepared to deviate if the person gives you details about a topic you had not considered. It's a good idea to actually talk to relatives at least twice: once when you first begin, then again after you have gathered quite a bit of research.

Divide Questions into Categories:

• Family history
• Childhood
• Youth
• Middle age
• Old age
• Narrator as parent
• Grandchildren
• Historical events
• General questions, thoughts, events during life, unusual life experiences,
• Personal philosophy and values
• Questions for interviewing Jewish, black and Hispanic relatives

FAMILY TREE 2

MATERIALS: *Design Originals Legacy Papers* (#0481 Teal linen, #0498 TeaDye tapestry, #0491 Coffee stripe)
• Acid-free adhesive
INSTRUCTIONS: Cut 3/4" strips of Coffee stripe paper. • Mat photos with TeaDye tapestry. • Adhere photos and mats to scrapbook page with Coffee strips underneath indicating family lineage.

The Green Family

Bob & Erma Green

Bob

Ray & Nina Brown

Janet

Bruce & Julie Green

Gabe

Jordan

Logan

Mike & Judy Arnot

Jackie

Tracy

Types of Questions to Ask:

- What were some of your grandfather's positive qualities?
- What about negative qualities?
- How did your grandparents meet?
- What was your grandfather's job?
- What's your fondest memory of your grandfather?
- What do you think he would have wanted to be remembered for? Why?
- As you think of your grandfather, how do you remember him looking?
- How old was he then?
- What did you call him?
- What did his wife, children and friends call him?
- Tell me a story about your father, son or grandfather that shows what kind of a man he was.

The next step will be to plan your research. You will need to write down what you know about the person you want to research and prioritize the resources that you want to use. It is good to schedule time to use the various resources you've identified.

You can gather more information on your family history by looking through family documents, photographs, love letters, laundry, receipts and old albums. You can search through birth, death, marriage and divorce records, in addition to civil, court and military records. Other places that are good to research are census and land records from all countries. You could also search through genealogical records in your home and visit libraries, archives and historical societies. There are also numerous sites that you can research online to gather more information about your family history. Check with your local Family History Centers for any additional information. You should verify all information you discover with census, vital or some other authoritative records.

You will need to make copies of source documents and store documents between acid-free paper and in a dark, dry and temperature consistent place. The best way to consolidate all your findings is by using a database to store and organize your information. Various programs (i.e. Family Tree Maker) can produce numerous reports specifically for family tree making.

GRANDPARENTS

MATERIALS: *Design Originals Legacy Papers* (#0490 Coffee linen, #0492 Coffee floral, #0502 Oval frame, #0503 Scroll frame)
- Cream parchment paper
- Acid-free adhesive

INSTRUCTIONS: Glue photos on frames. • Glue frames on scrapbook page. • Journal on parchment and glue on page.

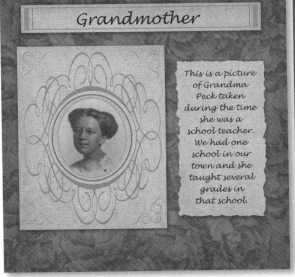

Grandmother

This is a picture of Grandma Peck taken during the time she was a school teacher. We had one school in our town and she taught several grades in that school.

Grandfathers

Here are four generations of our family. Holding Uncle Frank is Grandfather Ray. Standing, is Great Grandfather John, and on the left is Great, Great Grandfather Joe.

Make a Family Chart for the generations and relations in your family. These used to be recorded in the 'Family Bible'. Today memory albums are the best place to keep the chart of your family's history.

Start with a basic chart. Fill in the complete name, birth date, marriage date, decease date and where each person lived. Add names of babies and relatives by marriage. Add additional generations. Keep a copy of the charts in your lockbox. They contain valuable information.

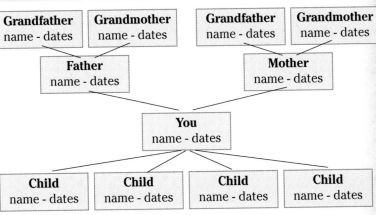

ON THE FRONT PORCH
by Renée Plains

MATERIALS: *Design Originals Legacy Papers* (#0500 TeaDye keys, #0490 Coffee Linen, #0495 Brown floral) • 2" x 4" piece of cardboard • Dark Brown markers for handwritten words • *Fiskars* alphabet stickers • *EK Success* rose squares • *Mrs. Grossman's* lace sticker • Rubber stamps (*Ma Vinci's* '1909'; *Rubbermoon* 'old photo'; *A Stamp in the Hand* large script) • *Goodies from Grandma* Small keys • Small jewelry tag • 24 gauge wire • Decorative scissors • Glue Dots • Acid-free adhesive

INSTRUCTIONS: Stamp large script stamp onto linen paper piece. • Cut a piece of linen paper to 12" x 5½". • Rubber stamp '1909' onto linen paper. Rubber stamp old photo onto small tag. • Glue a piece of floral paper to cardboard. • Assemble page. • Attach keys with wire. • Attach cardboard with Glue Dots.

SISTERS
by Renée Plains

MATERIALS: *Design Originals Legacy Papers* (#0499 TeaDye music, #0492 Coffee floral, #0485 Blue stripe, #0484 Blue linen) • *Making Memories* Tag • Rubber stamps (*Rubbermoon* 'Sisters'; *Hero Arts* #A2228 'Paraguay R') • 6 eyelets • 1 star nailhead • Stickers (*Scrapbook Borders* 'Sisters'; *Wordsworth* 'Sisters share...'; *Mrs. Grossman's* lace; *Pressed petals* flower) • *EK Success* flower tags • *DMC* Brown floss • Decorative scissors • Acid-free adhesive

INSTRUCTIONS: Stamp script words onto linen paper. • Cut the piece of linen paper to 6" x 7". Cut a piece of stripe to 12" x 4". Cut floral paper into a heart, about 5½" x 7" tall. • Rubber stamp 'Sisters' on the tag. Assemble pieces. • Cross stitch 5 'Xs' on the edge of the photo.

Add old objects to your page for that special touch.

MEMORIES
by Renée Plains

MATERIALS: *Design Originals Legacy Papers* (#0497 TeaDye letters, #0490 Coffee linen) • Font - *Three Island Press* Emily Austin and Broadsheet • *Hero Arts* 'c 1907' Printer's Type alphabet stamps • Star nailheads • Photocopies (page from McGuffey's First Reader, old report card and class picture) • *Scrapbook Borders* Memories sticker

INSTRUCTIONS: Photocopy (or print from a computer) script words onto linen paper (cut to a size that will fit your copier or printer).
• Cut the piece of linen paper to fit type. • Rubber stamp 'c 1907' onto linen paper and '1234567890' onto copy of old report card. • Glue copy of McGuffey's First Reader to letters paper. •Assemble page. Affix star nailheads on page.

TIP - Water-damaged photos will require the help of a conservator. But if photos are still wet, you can take a few steps to help salvage them. You first need to carefully separate water-soaked items and place them on a flat surface between layers of highly absorbent fabric. You can place flat, heavy objects on top of drying items to minimize curling and wrinkling.

Place water-soaked documents and photos in an air-conditioned room that has a temperature at or below 65 degrees to inhibit fungal growth, or use dehumidifiers and fans for a constant flow of air to expedite drying.

CHILDHOOD MEMORIES
by Renée Plains

MATERIALS: *Design Originals Legacy Papers* (#0498 TeaDye Tapestry, #0490 Coffee Linen, #0492 Coffee Floral, #0503 Scroll Frame) • *EK Success* Mini Fresh Cuts Days Gone By Tags • *Making Memories* eyelets • *American Tag Co.* antique mini brads

INSTRUCTIONS: Use tapestry paper for the background sheet. • Tear a 4$\frac{1}{2}$" x 12" piece of floral paper and adhere to bottom of page. • Cut out cuts and attach to page with eyelets. • Photocopy or print type on linen paper for the title and journaling and adhere with mini brads • Adhere photo and frame to page with acid-free adhesive.

Add tags or charms to your page.

YOUNG LOVE
by Renée Plains

MATERIALS: *Design Originals Legacy Papers* (#0498 TeaDye Tapestry, #0489 Rust Floral, #0488 Rust Stripe, #0487 Rust Linen, #0496 TeaDye Alphabet, #0497 TeaDye Letters) • Small button • *Limited Edition* #JV337H calendar stamp • *Sizzix* frame • Scallop Oval • Small and large heart punch • Glue Dots

INSTRUCTIONS: Use tapestry paper for the background sheet • Cut a 3" piece of striped paper and adhere to bottom of page • Attach border from alphabet paper to page above the striped paper • Cut a $\frac{1}{8}$" piece of striped paper and adhere $\frac{1}{2}$" from top of page • Cut out a large heart from floral paper and adhere to page. Adhere photo on top of heart. • Cut frame out of letters paper and adhere to page on top of photo • Stamp calendar stamp on tapestry paper • Photocopy or print type on linen and tapestry paper for title and journaling • Attach a button to page with a Glue Dot • Punch a large heart out of linen paper and attach to top left side of page • Punch two small hearts out of floral paper. Adhere to page.

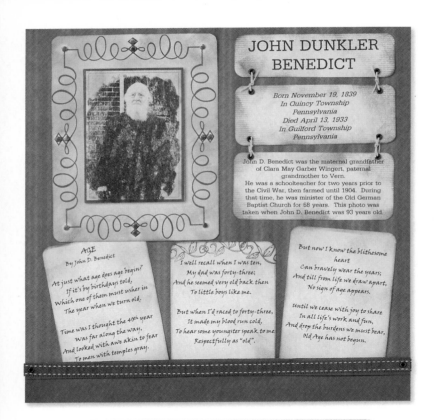

Age paper with chalk, coffee or ink. Add eyelets and twine to hang signs.

JOHN DUNKLER BENEDICT
by Carol Wingert

MATERIALS: *Design Originals Legacy Papers* (#0491 Coffee stripe, #0493 Brown linen, #0503 Scroll frame) • Eyelets • *Memory Lane* brads & ribbon • *Ranger* aging inks • *Magenta* Vine stamp

INSTRUCTIONS: Image transfer a heritage photo in the center of the frame. (See page 45 for image transfer instructions.) • Age by sponging on butterscotch and sepia inks. • Round corners of frame. • Add copper brads into swirls and on corners. • Computer generate title and journaling. • Age paper with inks. • Arrange photos and written panels on a 12" x 12" piece of striped paper. • Create a "pocket" on the bottom of the page to hold journaling cards. • Add ribbon and set with eyelets. • Set eyelets in title panels and tie together with waxed linen.

TIP - It is easy to age paper and stickers by painting with either chalking, coffee or walnut ink. Just use a sponge brush in either product to apply it right on the paper... around the edges looks best.

It is easy to achieve a darker color by painting several coats of the coffee or ink - let it dry in between. I dip tags (office supply type) right in a cup of the coffee then lay on a paper towel to dry.

Welcome to the beginning of a wonderful memory-making journey. Preserving your past for current and future generations is so very important.

ANNA KOLODIN-BABUSHKA
by Carol Wingert

MATERIALS: *Design Originals Legacy Papers* (#0498 TeaDye tapestry) • *7 gypsies* brass hardware • *7 gypsies* walnut ink • *Ink It!* brass frame • *Ink It!* leaves • *Loose Ends* fiber • *American Tag* Gold brads • *Anima Designs* brass tag • *Plaid* acrylic paint & crackle medium

INSTRUCTIONS: Adhere patterned paper to an 8" x 10" piece of chipboard. • Paint over paper with tan acrylic paint. Let dry. Brush surface with crackle medium. Allow to dry. • Apply a layer to tan paint sparingly over crackle medium. When dry, work in walnut ink with a finger over crackled areas. Sand off partial areas to create an aged look. • Mount photo on prepared board. Add fibers, leaves, buttons, title and brass tag. • Adhere board to 12" x 12" paper identical to that used on the board. • Thread ribbon through brass hardware and insert a tiny brass brad to hold in place. • Adhere ribbon and hardware to scrapbook page.

A MOTHER'S LEGACY

by Tim Holtz

MATERIALS: *Design Originals Legacy Papers* (#0487 Rust Linen, #0492 Coffee Floral, #0498 TeaDye Tapestry) • *Petersen Arne* vellum paper • *2 Peas in a Bucket* computer font • *A Lost Art* postcard stamp • *Ranger* Sepia archival ink pad • Glue Stick • *DMC* floss • Needle • Buttons • Craft Knife • Misc Embellishments (Pen Nib, Eyeglass Lens, Negatives, Lace) • *Beacon* Kid's Choice glue

INSTRUCTIONS: Start with tapestry paper. Tear pieces of floral paper for top and bottom of page, secure with glue stick. • Stamp linen paper with Archival Ink. Tear strips and glue to page. • Cut mat for photos leaving 1/2" around photo. • Using craft knife slit opposite corners of linen paper and slip corners of photos into them. • Tear a piece of vellum and stitch to corner of page with floss at random. • Print journaling on vellum and secure to page with buttons. • Add photos to page with acid-free adhesive. • Cut strips of negatives and adhere to page. Stitch buttons to page. Adhere lens, lace, and nib to page.

Get creative and add eyelets, elastic cord or fibers to complete your page.

A-B-C SCHOOL DAYS

by Carol Wingert

MATERIALS: *Design Originals Legacy Papers* (#0489 Rust Floral, #0487 Rust linen, #0497 TeaDye letters, #0496 TeaDye alphabet) • *7 gypsies* Black elastic & watch face • *Making Memories* metal rimmed tags • *Ranger* aging ink • *Clearsnap* Ancient Page stamping ink • Rubber stamps (*Limited Edition* numbers; *Green Pepper Press* background)

INSTRUCTIONS: Tear a piece of 8 1/2" x 11" corrugated paper around the edges. • Set eyelets with reinforcements on the left side. Add elastic. • Cut out alphabet blocks and adhere to square tags. Outline with rust ink. • Stamp numbers on a strip of Rust linen paper. Adhere school photo to cardboard. Create a corner "slip" out of the numbers strip. • Using 2 standard manila tags, create a gatefold book and cover with letters paper. Set 2 eyelets with reinforcements. Journal inside the book and add a watch face which resembles a school clock. Tie book together with linen thread. • Adhere corrugated panel to page. Adhere the tag book under photo.

Adhere a decorative book with a personal message inside to your page for that special touch.

*Preserving the past,
recording the
present and looking
to the future;
these memories create
a treasure book of
a family's legacy.*

BONNER WEDDING *by Laura Gregory*
MATERIALS: *Design Originals Legacy Papers* (#0480 Green floral, #0479 Green stripe) • *Stop N Crop* fiber • *Westrim* heart nailheads • *Jolee* flower corners • Provo Craft Laser letter stickers • Acid-free adhesive
INSTRUCTIONS: Tear a 2" x 12" strip of floral paper and adhere to the page. • Fold an 18" strip of fiber in half, twist it together and attach to the page with nailheads. • Adhere the photo to the page and add photo corners. • Apply letter stickers to the page.

SISTERS   *by Christy Lemond*
MATERIALS: *Design Originals Legacy Papers* (#0499 TeaDye music, #0480 Green floral, #0495 Brown floral, #0494 Brown stripe) • Vellum • *Karen Foster* mini brads • *EK Success* fresh tags • *Creative Imaginations* large eyelets •

Acid-free adhesive
INSTRUCTIONS: Tear a 2½" x 11" strip of striped paper. • Attach to page with eyelets. • Adhere the tag and title. • Attach journal block to the page with brads. • Double mat photos and glue to the page.

Every Wedding
is an Important Legacy

Memories, photos, images and mementos add up to bring importance to our Legacy. Preserving your past for current and for future generations is important.

Start your journey with elegant Legacy Scrapbook Papers, Frames and Legacy Cuts. The coordinated color scheme and understated designs make creating fashionable pages enjoyable and nearly effortless! Everything coordinates, no matter what you choose!

Every person, every event, every memory... all together these add up to... who we are, who came before us, why we are here, and where we came from. They even delineate where our family is going.

THE CAKE
by Ruth Ann Warwick

MATERIALS: *Design Originals Legacy Papers* (#0483 Teal floral, #0481 Teal linen, #0508 Floral Cuts) • Vellum • Gold paper • Acid-free adhesive

INSTRUCTIONS: Tear a 2$1/2$" strip of Teal linen to create the left border. • Cut out the square Floral Cuts. • Adhere a 2" x 12" vellum strip and a $3/8$" strip of gold paper on top. • Adhere the vertical torn strip to cover edges of vellum. • Mat photos and adhere to the page. Adhere floral cuts to the page.

OUR RINGS
by Ruth Ann Warwick

MATERIALS: *Design Originals Legacy Papers* (#0483 Teal floral, #0481 Teal linen) • Vellum • *Robin's Nest* Printed vellum • Gold paper • Candle charms • Acid-free adhesive

INSTRUCTIONS: Cut an 8" square of vellum. • Cut a 2" x 12" leaves vellum strip and a $3/8$" gold paper strip. • Cut a 4" x 9" rectangle of leaves vellum.• Using an acid-free adhesive, lightly press the adhesive to the page where you are going to place the 8" square. Let the adhesive almost dry, and gently lay the vellum down. Do not press the vellum down firmly on the page. Do it lightly. Adhere the vellum strips. • Adhere a photo to the rectangle vellum and then to the page, hiding the adhesive under the photo. • Now add any any embellishments.

KAITLYN
by Delores Frantz

MATERIALS: *Design Originals Legacy Papers* (#0481 Teal linen, #0482 Teal stripe, #0483 Teal floral) • Ivory cardstock • 18" of Ivory 1" ribbon • 27" of Ivory 3/4" braid with pearls • *Provo Craft* Ivory 1 1/8" Laser letters • Pop Dots • *Fiskars* scallop scissors • 3" circle template

INSTRUCTIONS: Cover album page with floral paper. • Cut photo into a 3" circle. Cut a 6 5/8" heart from stripe paper, and a 9 1/4" heart from linen paper. Glue photo and hearts to cardstock. Cut around shapes with scallop scissors. • Arrange and stack shapes on floral paper. Attach each layer to the one below it with Pop Dots. • Glue bow, letters and braid to page.

Memories, photos and mementos add up to bring importance to our Legacy.

PRINCESS MARLEY
by Susan Keuter

MATERIALS: *Design Originals Legacy Papers* (#0482 Teal stripe, #0483 Teal floral) • *Bazzill* Cardstock • *Marvy* Mega Giga square punch • Computer Fonts - Platthand Demo, Notehand Regular

INSTRUCTIONS: Use light-colored cardstock as album page • Cut two 6" squares from Black cardstock • Photocopy or print journaling on floral paper and cut into two 5 1/2" squares. Mount to Black cardstock. • Cut two 5 1/2" squares from striped paper. • Cut 8 photos with a square punch and mount 4 each in the center of the striped paper squares.

TAKE TO THE SKIES
by Tim Holtz

MATERIALS: *Design Originals Legacy Papers* (#0481 Teal linen, #0482 Teal stripe) • *Petersen Arne* Light and Dark Teal cardstock • *American Tag* shipping tags • *2 Peas in a Bucket* font • *Ranger* Adirondack inkers (Stream, Bottle, Espresso) • *Making Memories* eyelets • *Stanislaus* plane charm • Map scrap • Glue stick • Scissors • Mounting tape • *Zig* Dark Teal & Black S/B Marker • *Beacon* Kid's Choice glue

INSTRUCTIONS: Tear linen paper in half and crumple up half of paper. Tear a strip of stripe paper for center of page. • Mount papers to cardstock using an acid-free adhesive and trim 6 1/2" of Legacy papers to fit cardstock. • Mount photos on dark teal cardstock. • Print titles and journaling onto light teal cardstock. • Trim around page and journal with S/B marker using a wavy line. • Mount journal and titles to dark teal cardstock and secure with eyelets. • Spray tags with Adirondack inkers and let dry • Write names using black S/B marker. • Glue map scrap to page. • Mount titles, photos, tags, and journal to page using mounting tape. • Glue charm to page.

Auntie Em page with the photo frame flaps closed and tied securely with a satin ribbon.

Place a strip of satin ribbon behind the fold-out framed photo. Untie the ribbon when you open the top and bottom flaps.

Retie the ribbon in a romantic bow or knot when the flaps are folded shut.

AUNTIE EM
by Shannon Smith

MATERIALS: *Design Originals Legacy Papers* (#0482 Teal Stripe, #0483 Teal Floral, #0481 Teal Linen) • *The Papercut* (vellum and parchment paper) • Button • *Offray* ribbon • *Fiskars* paper trimmer • Gold Embellishments - *Boutique Trims, Inc* and *Jesse James Buttons* • Teal Metallic Rub-On • Old photo in frame • *Tombow* Paper glue

INSTRUCTIONS: Print title on vellum. • Wrinkle and flatten out parchment paper and tear edges to desired size. Glue vellum title to parchment paper and top with button and ribbon. Adhere to page. • Open old photo holder and take out picture and frame. Line the inside of the frame with paper, replace photo and frame, glue in place. • Print out story on parchment paper and adhere to bottom flap of holder. • Decorate with gold embellishments. • Close holder and tie shut with ribbon. • While the holder is shut, attach it and ribbon to the page. • Rub on metallic to the seal on the front of the holder.

Open the top and bottom flaps to reveal Auntie's photo!

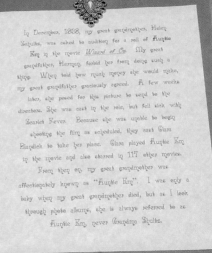

In December, 1938, my great grandmother, Helen Schultz, was asked to audition for a roll of Auntie Em in the movie *Wizard of Oz*. My great grandfather, Herman, forbid her from doing such a thing. When told how much money she would make, my great grandfather graciously agreed. A few weeks later, she posed for this picture to send to the directors. She was cast in the role, but fell sick with Scarlet Fever. Because she was unable to begin shooting the film as scheduled, they cast Clara Blandick to take her place. Clara played Auntie Em in the movie and also starred in 117 other movies.

From then on, my great grandmother was affectionately known as "Auntie Em". I was only a baby when my great grandmother died, but as I look through photo albums, she is always referred to as Auntie Em, never Grandma Shultz.

Greeting Cards and Gifts

Can Become a Legacy too

GREETING CARDS
by Renée Plains

BASIC INSTRUCTIONS: Cut cardstock $5^1/2$" x $8^1/2$", score at the center an fold with bone folder. • Cut a piece of Legacy paper with deckle scissors $1/4$" x 4" for background. Glue to center front of card. Use Xyron to appl adhesive to the background paper. • Make envelope using the *Kreate-a-lop* size A2 standard invitation envelope and paper. Follow the template direc tions to tear and fold the paper. Stamp the gridded inside with a scrip stamp and color with chalk or stamp pad ink and a stipple brush. • Puncl out a small heart or star and glue to inside flap of envelope.

SWEET FRIEND
by Renée Plains

MATERIALS: *Design Originals Legacy Papers* (#0492 Coffee floral, #049 Coffee linen, #0488 Rust stripe) • Brown card • Scrap of Cream paper • Rubber stamps (*Stampa Rosa Inc* G59-181 script stamp; *Acey Deuc* 'Come Hither' #K1-843 script; *Inkadinkadoo/Dawn Houser* Sentiment: Collection 'Wishing you the happiest of days' #8517A) • *Kreate-a-lope*
INSTRUCTIONS:
Cut a $2^1/2$" x $2^3/4$" rectangle from linen paper. Stamp script stamp on paper • Cut a piece of stripe paper $2^1/2$" x $1^3/4$". Tear one side to make the rec tangle $2^1/2$" x $1^1/4$". Stamp script stamp and glue to bottom of rectangle then adhere to center of card. • Cut a small picture (1" x $1^1/8$") and glue tc stamped rectangle. Type or stamp 'sweet friend' on cream paper. Cut ou and glue under picture. • Stamp 'Wishing you the happiest of days' inside card. • Make envelope with linen paper.

TIME FLIES
by Renée Plains

MATERIALS: *Design Originals Legacy Papers* (#0501 TeaDye clocks, #0487 Rust linen, #0492 Coffee floral) • Gold card • Rubber stamps (*Limited Edition* JV337H calendar; *Rubbermoon* 'time flies'; *Zettiology* label) • Brown & White stamp pads • Clock face • Heart punch • Photocopy of lady • Photocopy of wings • *Zig* brown writer • *Kreate-a-lope* • Glue Dots
INSTRUCTIONS: Cut a rectangle of linen paper 3" x $2^1/8$". Stamp Calendar stamp with white ink. Glue paper to card. • Cut out a picture of a lady and wings. Glue to rectangle. • Use glue dots to place watch face on card. Use picture of card as a guide for placement. • Stamp "time flies" and label stamp on floral paper. Cut out and glue in place on card. • Punch out a heart from linen paper and glue on label. • Write 2003 with ZIG brown writer. • Make envelope.

TRICK OR TREAT
by Renée Plains

MATERIALS: *Design Originals Legacy Papers* (#0478 Green linen, #0479 Green stripe, #0506 Halloween Cuts) • Black card • Alphabet stamp set • Black ink pad • *7Gypsies* script paper • Star nailheads • *Kreate-a-lope*
INSTRUCTIONS: Use script paper for background paper. • Cut three Pumpkin Cuts. Set a star nailhead on each cut. Glue cuts to card. • Stamp 'Trick or Treat' with an alphabet set on linen paper. Use black chalk to age paper. Use picture of card as a guide for placement. Glue to card. • Stamp 'Happy Halloween' on linen paper. Use black chalk to age paper. Cut out and glue in place inside card. • Make envelope. Cut out Pumpkin cut and glue to envelope flap.

CHRISTMAS GREETINGS
by Renée Plains

MATERIALS: *Design Originals Legacy Papers* (#0478 Green linen, #0504 Holiday Cuts) • Ready made cream card and envelope • Rubber stamps (*Stampers Anonymous* script; *Rubbermoon* 'merry christmas'; *A Stamp in The Hand* script) • Red ink pad • *Kreate-a-lope* • Decorative scissors
INSTRUCTIONS: Use linen paper for background paper. • Stamp script stamp with red ink on cream paper. Cut a $2^1/4$" x $2^1/2$" rectangle from this paper and glue to card. • Cut Christmas greeting with postage decorative paper scissors. Glue to card. • Stamp 'merry christmas' on inside of card. • Stamp script stamp on envelope with red ink. • Make envelope and stamp 'merry christmas' along top edge of envelope. Cut a Holiday Cut and glue to envelope flap.

ACCORDION HEART BOOK

by Renée Plains

MATERIALS: *Design Originals Legacy Papers* (#0495 Brown floral, #0490 Coffee linen, #0497 TeaDye letters, #0492 Coffee floral, #0487 Rust linen, #0488 Rust stripe) • Black poster board • Script stamps; *Rubbermoon* 'remembering' stamp • Small pictures (*Stampa Rosa* Collage-ables & Vintage Photos) • Star nailheads • Tarnished thin copper • 28 gauge wire • Heart punch • 18" of $1/4$" silk ribbon • $1 1/2$" Heart punch

INSTRUCTIONS: Cut black poster board 3" x 18". Score at 3" intervals for folding. Start folding from center matching ends. Fold at next scoring line back to center on both ends. Fold last fold on each side matching up ends. Use a bone folder at each fold for a nice sharp crease. • Cut two pieces of cardboard 3" square. Cut two floral $3 1/2$" squares. Cover the cardboard squares folding edges towards back. • Cut ten $2 3/4$" squares from an assortment of papers. Stamp the squares with script stamps and words. Glue a picture to each square adding dates, labels or strips of paper to collage each square. • Glue a collaged square to each page of the accordion book except the outside covers. • Glue center of ribbon across the middle (horizontal) of the back cover. Glue a cover over ribbon. • Tear a $2 1/2$" paper square and stamp a script stamp on paper. Glue to front cover. • Punch a large heart from copper and wrap wire around the heart. Glue to front cover. • Stamp 'remembering' on paper and cut out, then glue under heart. • Glue front cover to book. Tie ribbon across front cover.

Fold up this darling Accordion Heart book then tie it with a romantic ribbon. This miniature photo album makes a perfect memento or gift.

XOXO

by Renée Plains

MATERIALS: *Design Originals Legacy Paper #0489* Rust floral • Rust card • *7 gypsies* script paper • Brass oval tag AB676 (www.artchixstudio.com) • Rubber stamps (*Rubbermoon* 'xoxo'; *Hero Arts* #A2126 heart; *Inkadinkadoo/Dawn Houser* Sentiments Collection #8517A 'thinking of you') • $1/8$" silver eyelets • *Stazon* black ink • Glue Dots • Decorative scissors

INSTRUCTIONS: Cut a heart from script paper using small scallop decorative scissors. Glue to center of card. • Cut a small oval picture ($1 3/4$" x $1 1/4$") with deckle decorative paper scissors and glue to heart. • Stamp 'xoxo' with black ink on oval brass tag. • Place eyelets through holes and set eyelets. • Adhere label under picture with Glue Dots. • Stamp 'thinking of you' on inside of card. • Stamp heart on tan paper, cut out square and glue above saying inside card. • Make envelope with floral paper.

TIP - It is easy to get a fairly straight tear by placing a plastic ruler along the edge to be torn and pulling the paper up. If it is torn from the wrong side (gridded side of paper), the edge will have color right up to the torn edge. If you tear it from the right side, there will be lots of white paper along the torn edge. Use chalk along the edge to cover any white that you may wish to hide.

ENOUGH SAID
by Susan Keuter

MATERIALS: *Design Originals Legacy Papers* (#0478 Green linen, #0479 Green stripe) • *Bazzill* cardstock • *Creative Impressions* gold square brads • Date stamp • *twopeasinabucket.com* 2Peas Arizona font • Computer Fonts - Oldstyle Typewriter , Girls are Weird, Mufferaw • Hermafix Transfer • Sewing Machine

INSTRUCTIONS: Use linen paper as album page. • Cut 3" of striped paper. • Cut a 1 1/2" piece of light cardstock, mount under left side of 3" of striped paper. Cut a 1 1/2" piece of Black cardstock, mount under right side of 3" of striped paper • Cut up scraps and use Hermafix Transfer adhesive to place all the small scraps of paper onto the stripe paper. Machine stitch through all scraps on striped paper. • Cut a 7 3/4" x 5" piece of light cardstock. Cut a 5 1/2" x 5" piece of dark cardstock and mount on light cardstock. Mount photo on cardstock pieces • Cut a 7 3/4" x 2 3/4" piece of another light cardstock, mount under other cardstock.

GRAND CANYON   (title in metal letters)
by Susan Keuter

MATERIALS: *Design Originals Legacy Papers* (#0494 Brown stripe, #0497 TeaDye letters) • *Bazzill* cardstock • *Bazzill* heavyweight vellum • *Timeless Touches* Autumn Leaves fibers • *Scrap Works* nailhead frames • *Making Memories* metal letters • *Stampin' Up* Copper embossing powder • *SF Scribbled Sans* computer font • Pop Dots

INSTRUCTIONS: Use striped paper as album page. • Print journaling on 2 7/8" x 10 1/4" piece of vellum and adhere to left side of page. • Tear a 12" x 2 1/2" strip of dark cardstock and adhere 2 3/4" from bottom of page. • Cut two 4 1/4" x 7 1/4" pieces of light cardstock and mount a photo on each piece. • Emboss the metal letters and frames with embossing powder. • Affix metal letters to page. • Add cuts of index prints from the photo lab for the pictures inside the 6 nailhead frames. Place Pop Dots behind the photographs before affixing the frames to the page to keep the pictures raised. • Add fibers to page.

It's never too late to start a scrapbook!

Use metal letters to make the theme of your page stand out.

the GRAND CANYON
by Susan Keuter

MATERIALS: *Design Originals Legacy Papers* (#0491 Coffee stripe, #0487 Rust linen) • Cardstock - DMD, Bazzill • Fibers • *twopeasinabucket.com* brass label holder • *Clipola* paper clips • *Rings and Things* Arizona charm • *Craf-T* chalk • *Stampin' Up* Gold embossing powder • Computer Fonts - Onyx, Dear Joe Italic • Cash register receipt • Tacky Tape

INSTRUCTIONS: Use light cardstock as album page. • Cut a 12" x 5 1/2" piece of striped paper and adhere to bottom of page. • Cut a 12" x 4" piece of Black cardstock and mount above striped paper. • Cut two 4" x 7" pieces of Black cardstock and mount photos to the cardstock. • Cut two 4 1/4" x 8 1/2" pieces of the light cardstock and print journaling on each piece. Mount one matted photo on each piece about 1/8" from the top. Tear the bottom of the light cardstock and apply embossing powder on edges. • Print title on a 2 7/8" x 1 1/2" piece of light cardstock and shade with chalk. Slip title piece in brass label holder. Attach two pieces of hemp to each side of holder and secure ends with tape. • Add a cash register receipt and a piece of torn paper with a small photo and charm to page with paper clips.

Favorite Memories

Add interesting family history and tell the story about your favorite photos. Accent your pages with decorative fibers.

THE HANDS OF TIME

by Susan Keuter

MATERIALS: *Design Originals Legacy Papers* (#0501 TeaDye clocks, #0490 Coffee linen) • *Bazzill* Cardstock • *Timeless Touches* Autumn Leaves fibers • *Scrap Works* Waxy Flax • Hemp • *Accu-Cut* tag die-cut • *7 gypsies* photo corners • *Fancifuls, Inc.* watch charm • *Hero Arts* alphabet stamps • *Stampin' Up* Close to Cocoa ink pad

INSTRUCTIONS: Use dark cardstock as album page. • Print journaling on a 3" piece of linen paper and mount to left side of page leaving a $1/8$" border on the left, top and bottom sides. • Cut a $8^1/2$" piece of clock paper and mount to right side of page leaving a $1/8$" border on the right, top and bottom sides. • Mount photo to $8^1/8$" x $6^1/8$" piece of dark cardstock. • Take two 6" pieces of dark cardstock. Fold 1" of the cardstock down on each piece and then place the folded edge at the top of the tag die-cut before cutting. • Enlarge your photograph on a color copier and use a square punch to punch out the hands from the photograph. • Finish out tags with fibers and stamps. • Adhere all pieces to page.

BEST FRIENDS

by Susan Keuter

MATERIALS: *Design Originals Legacy Papers* (#0488 Rust stripe, #0487 Rust linen, #0489 Rust floral, #0497 TeaDye letters) • *Bazzill* Cardstock • *Timeless Touches* Autumn Leaves fibers • *Scrap Works* waxy flax • *Stampin' Up* shrink plastic heart charm • *Stampin' Up* Gold embossing powder • *Emagination* heart punch • Date stamp • Sewing machine

INSTRUCTIONS: Use striped paper as album page. • Weave fourteen $1/2$" strips of floral paper and ten $1/2$" strips of linen paper together and mount on cardstock. Mount cardstock to upper right side of page under photo. • Cut a piece of $7^1/2$" dark cardstock for photo mat. Adhere photo to mat. Stamp date on mat. • Print journaling on light cardstock. Cut a piece of $6^1/8$" light cardstock and mount on a $6^1/2$" dark cardstock. Connect to matted photo with waxy flax. • Create a $7^1/4$" tag from letters paper, add 7" piece of journaling on light cardstock. Machine stitch to finish out. • Add fibers and heart charm to tag.

Quick Little Gifts

PAPER COVERED JOURNALS
by Renée Plains

INSTRUCTIONS: Cut a piece of Legacy paper just slightly larger than the cover. Take advantage of the TeaDyed edges by lining this edge up at the black binding edge. • Paint PVA glue on cover and lay the paper on the glue, smoothing with a brayer. • Turn the cover to the wrong side and trim the excess paper with scissors or an X-Acto knife. Repeat for back cover.

Adorn a little journal or booklets with a fast and easy wire and button closure.

JOURNAL
by Renée Plains

MATERIALS: *Design Originals Legacy Paper* #0497 TeaDye letters • Small composition book • 24 gauge wire • Small button • Key charm • *Zettiology* label stamp • *Zig* .005 Millennium black pen • *Books by Hand* PVA adhesive

INSTRUCTIONS: Cover journal with paper. • Stamp label and write "journal" with a Zig pen. Cut out label and glue in place on cover. • Cut a piece of wire and thread one end through button. Wrap end around wire to secure. Place wire around journal and thread other end through button. Pull the wire tight around book and about an inch from the button, add the key charm to the wire. Leaving the inch of wire will allow the wire to be easily loosened to pull off the journal and open it up.

WHAT A FRIEND
by Renée Plains

MATERIALS: *Design Originals Legacy Paper* #0499 TeaDye music • Small composition book • Small picture of girl • 24 gauge wire • Small button • *ARTchix Studio* #AB575 mini brass nameplates • *Rubbermoon* 'xoxo' rubber stamp • *StazOn* ink • *Books by Hand* PVA adhesive

INSTRUCTIONS: Cover journal with paper. • Stamp 'xoxo' on mini brass nameplate with StazOn ink and glue in place on cover. Glue picture above nameplate. • Cut a piece of wire and thread one end through button from back and then out to back. Wrap end around wire to secure. Place wire around journal and wrap wire around button to hold in place.

1917 JOURNAL
by Renée Plains

MATERIALS: *Design Originals Legacy Paper* #0486 Blue floral • Small composition book • Small picture of girl • 12" of 1/4" wide ribbon • Small square of cream text weight paper • Small square of text paper (try the stocks and bonds section of newspaper) • *Zig* .005 Millennium black pen • *Books by Hand* PVA adhesive

INSTRUCTIONS: Cover journal with paper. • Glue picture on the slightly larger text paper square and glue to cover. Write 'c 1917' on text weight paper with pen. Glue below picture. Chalk edges of picture and 1917 with brown and black decorating chalk. • Tie ribbon around journal.

LARGE JOURNAL
by Renée Plains

MATERIALS: *Design Originals Legacy Papers* (#0495 Brown floral, #0494 Brown stripe) • Large composition book • *Books by Hand* PVA adhesive • 36" of 1/2" wide ribbon

INSTRUCTIONS: Cover journal with paper. • Cut 1/2" strip of the striped paper for trim on the journal. Glue along black binding tape. • Tie ribbon around journal.

TIME'S LEGACY JOURNAL

by Tim Holtz

MATERIALS: *Design Originals Legacy Papers* (#0501 TeaDye clocks, #0495 Brown floral) • *DCC* Brown journal • *Making Memories* metal letter eyelets • *Postmodern Design* walnut ink • *US ArtQuest* Mica Tile • *US ArtQuest* Silver foil tape • Pocket watch • Chain • Rusty key • Metal corners • Journal scrap • Wire • Glue Stick • Craft Knife • Ruler • Scissors • *Beacon* Kid's Choice glue

INSTRUCTIONS: Using a ruler and craft knife, cut out a window into journal to fit watch. • Lay clock paper face down. • Apply glue stick to outside cover of journal. Lay over top of paper and crease edges around spine of journal. • Cut an "X" inside of window and turn edges of paper inside. Trim around journal leaving about $1/2$" to fold over. Turn edges over to inside of journal to secure. • Cut a strip of floral paper for spine of journal and glue it. • Add silver foil tape to cover of journal. • Glue journal scrap to inside of window with glue stick. Glue pocket watch to inside of window on journal. • Glue metal corners, mica, and metal letters to journal. • Add wire to side of journal for clasp and add rusty key to close. • Paint edges of journal pages with walnut ink, let dry.

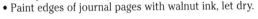

Add a collection of charms and game pieces to write titles and words.

DREAM JOURNAL - COVER

by Carol Wingert

MATERIALS: *Design Originals Legacy Papers* (#0480 Green floral, #0478 Green linen, #0492 Coffee floral, #0498 TeaDye tapestry) • *7 gypsies* gatefold journal • *7 gypsies* nickel spine handles • *ARTchix* mirror tiles • *Stampendous* Letter Stickers • Collage card • Fibers • *Stampington & Co.* bendable art • *Ranger* aging ink • *Plaid* Mod Podge • Brayer • E6000 glue • Adhesive

INSTRUCTIONS: Tear the papers to resemble water and sand. Adhere to front of gatefold journal. Edge with a torn piece of patterned tan paper. Adhere purchased art card 'into the waves'. • Roller cover with a brayer to remove air bubbles. Allow to dry. • When dry, apply matte Mod Podge with foam brush, stippling the surface before it dries. Repeat the process until you have completed 5 layers. • Add fibers and bendable art shell. • Apply sticker letters to the mirror tiles and adhere tiles to the face of the journal with industrial glue. • Adhere the "handles" to the cover with E6000 glue.

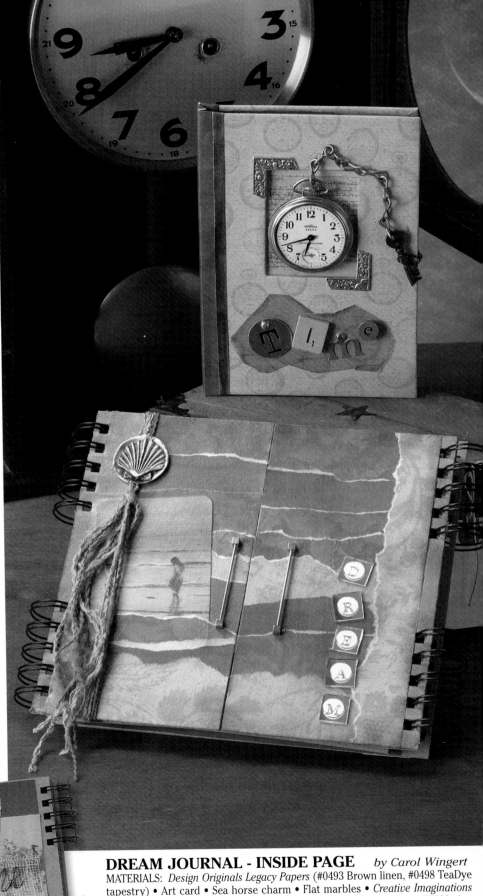

DREAM JOURNAL - INSIDE PAGE   *by Carol Wingert*

MATERIALS: *Design Originals Legacy Papers* (#0493 Brown linen, #0498 TeaDye tapestry) • Art card • Sea horse charm • Flat marbles • *Creative Imaginations* "treasure" wire • *Loose Ends* fiber paper • *Loose Ends* fiber ribbon • E6000 glue • Adhesive

INSTRUCTIONS: Adhere solid paper to journal page. • Adhere a torn piece at the bottom to create a border. • Add 3 glass puddles and adhere with E6000. • Wire charm to wire word. Attach word to fiber ribbon and fiber paper. • Insert purchased art card. Adhere to face of page.

A father is someone you look up to No matter how tall you grow.

TED HOFSISS

TED HOFSISS
by Ruth Ann Warwick

MATERIALS: *Design Originals Legacy Papers* (#0478 Green linen, #0479 Green stripe) • Natural color paper • Eyelets • Hemp • *Stop N Crop* wrought iron die-cuts • *Stop N Crop* tiles • Glue Dots
INSTRUCTIONS: Tear a $2^1/_2$" x 12" strip and glue across the top of the page. • Tear a rectangle 5" x $1^1/_2$" and cut a journal block $4^1/_2$" x 1"; set eyelets in each corner. • Trace the tag and then tear around it and add jute. • Adhere the tiles and rustic die-cuts with Glue Dots.

Legacy Papers are positively mistake proof. You will be proud of every page you create!

VACATIONS

PARADISE

MAUI

Jeanne and John

Pineapple FARM

half way to Hana

Ocean SEA
Snorkling
STAR FRUIT
Pineapple
sugar cane
HANA
waterfall
sea shells
MANGO
Luau
Hilo Hattie
whale
watching
BoogiE BoARD
orchids

1991

HAWAII

MAUI
by Renée Plains

MATERIALS: *Design Originals Legacy Papers* (#0479 Green stripe, #0490 Coffee linen) • *Making Memories* pewter snaps • Die-cut letters • Rubber stamps (*All Night Media* Ransom alphabet; *Susan Branch* numbers) • *Susan Branch* 'Vacations' sticker • Acid-free adhesive • Black pen
INSTRUCTIONS: Use linen paper for the background sheet. • Cut a $4^3/_4$" x 12" piece of striped paper and adhere to left side of page. • Cut out four photos and adhere to striped paper with acid-free adhesive. • Stamp title on striped paper. • Cut two $3^1/_2$" x $^1/_4$" strips and two $5^1/_2$" x $^1/_4$" strips from striped paper. Use the strips to make a frame around large photo and place snaps on 4 corners. • Adhere die-cut letters to page for title. • Place sticker vertically on upper left hand side of page. • Journal by each photo with Black pen.

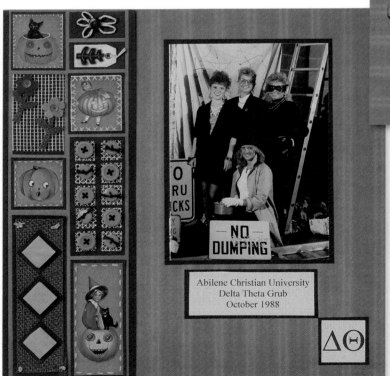

O
R U
CKS
YG
IG

NO
DUMPING

Abilene Christian University
Delta Theta Grub
October 1988

ΔΘ

Add quick Legacy 'Cuts'.

Tie on buttons with floss.

 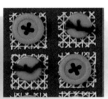

SORORITY
by Laura Gregory

MATERIALS: *Design Originals Legacy Papers* (#0478 Green linen, #0479 Green stripe, #0506 Halloween Cuts) • Black cardstock • *Magic Mesh* • Tiles • Burlap • Buttons • *Jolee's Boutique* felt flowers • *DMC* floss
INSTRUCTIONS: To make the color blocking border, cut a 4" border for your background. • Cut out the Pumpkin Cuts and mat them. Glue the cuts sporadically on the border strip. • Fill in the remaining spaces with additional embellishments.

WREATH Scrapbook Page

by Delores Frantz

MATERIALS: *Design Originals Legacy Papers* (#0498 TeaDye tapestry, #0478 Green linen, 2 #0480 Green floral) • Vellum • 4 Red *Offray* ribbon flowers (or make your own with ribbon) • 9 Red ⁵⁄₈" buttons • 18" of Red ⁵⁄₈" ribbon • Pop Dots • 28 Gold beads • *Fiskars* corkscrew scissors

INSTRUCTIONS: Cover album page with tapestry paper. Cut and glue narrow borders. Glue photo to center of page. • Using roses as a guide, cut a 10" circle of floral paper with a 5" opening at the center. Glue over photo. • Cut 12 rose designs from floral paper. Arrange 6 rose cutouts around photo. Attach to page with Pop Dots. Arrange remaining roses on top of first roses and attach with Pop Dots. • Glue flowers, buttons and bow to wreath. • Journal words on vellum and glue to page.

Dress up your simple wreath. Shape red ribbon into poinsettias. Add buttons and a bow.

1. Cut ribbon into six 1³⁄₄" pieces for petals.

2. Fold ribbon.

3. Fold again.

4. Pinch ribbon and stitch.

5. Pinch and string 6 petals on thread.

6. Pull thread tight and add 7 Gold beads.

7. Coil the beads to make flower center.

8. To anchor beads, tack between with thread. Take thread to back and tie off.

'FAMILY' Album Cover

by Carol Wingert

MATERIALS: *Design Originals Legacy Papers* (#0479 Green stripe, #0480 Green floral, #0504 Holiday Cuts) • *7 gypsies* porcelain "Family" medallion • *Making Memories* metal rimmed tag • *On The Surface* fibers • Adhesive

INSTRUCTIONS: To create a book cover, sew sueded paper on the spine edge of a piece of printed paper. • Adhere to a piece of 8" x 10" bookboard. • Miter the corners at a 45° angle and fold to the back of the cover. Glue in place. • Adhere photos and journaling to a coordinating piece of paper and machine stitch around the edges with a decorative stitch. Adhere to face of cover. • Cut suede triangles to fit corners and machine stitch inner edge. Adhere to corners. • Adhere Christmas cut to the inside of the tag. • Tie fibers to book edge. Tie tag to fibers. • Insert 2 mini brads in medallion holes. Adhere to the cover with industrial glue.

Frames and Mats for Photos

PICTURE MATS IN FRAMES *by Renée Plains*
INSTRUCTIONS: Use a purchased mat or double mat that fits your frame. If using a double mat separate them carefully so that they can be covered separately. Cut paper slightly larger than mat. • Paint PVA glue on mat (if there is a beveled edge turn it over and use the straight cut side - it is easier to trim with this side) and lay paper on mat smoothing with a brayer. • Lay mat with the front down and cut an "X" from inside corners using a sharp X-Acto knife. • Cut along inside edges with X-Acto knife and remove paper. Trim outside edges following along edge.

2003 MAT *by Renée Plains*
MATERIALS: *Design Originals Legacy Papers* (#0489 Rust Floral paper, #0488 Rust stripe, #0490 Coffee linen) • Pewter eyelets • *Zettiology* label stamp • Heart punch • Copper sheet tarnished with Liver of Sulphur • *ZIG* writer • Adhesive
INSTRUCTIONS: Cover outer mat with floral paper. • Cut $5/8$" strips from stripe paper. • Glue strips to inside edges and miter corners. • Set eyelets at corners of inner mat. Glue double mat together. • Stamp label on linen paper. • Punch a heart from copper sheet. Glue label and heart to mat. • Write year on label.

STAR MAT *by Renée Plains*
MATERIALS: *Design Originals Legacy Papers* (#0486 Blue floral, #0488 Rust stripe, #0547 Dictionary) • Pewter eyelets • *Making Memories* small round metal rimmed tag • Star nailhead • Adhesive
INSTRUCTIONS: Cover mat with floral paper. • Cut $3/8$" strips from stripe paper. Glue strips to inside edges. • Set eyelets at corners of inner strips. • Glue dictionary paper to tag and trim with an X-Acto knife at metal edge. • Set star nailhead at center of tag. Glue to top of mat.

Add details with coins, stamps and eyelets.

FOAM CORE MOUNTS
by Renée Plains
INSTRUCTIONS: Cut a piece of foam core 3" x $3^1/_2$". • Cover edges with tarnished copper foil tape folding over on each side. • Glue a slightly smaller piece of paper to both sides of foam core. • Cover both sides of a $2^1/_2$" x 3" piece of cardboard. • Cut out stand using template. Glue to center back of frame after front is finished.

SWEET BABY
by Renée Plains
MATERIALS: *Design Originals Legacy Papers* (#0486 Blue floral, #0495 Brown floral) • Foam core • Small picture • Slide mount • Copper eyelets • *Zettiology* label stamp • Star nailhead • *Zig* .005 Millennium pen • Tarnished copper foil tape • Adhesive
INSTRUCTIONS: Make frame. • Cover slide mount with floral paper. • Stamp script stamp on slide. • Glue picture behind slide mount. • Set eyelets at each corner of slide mount. Glue to frame. • Stamp label on floral paper. Write 'sweet baby' in label. Cut out and glue below slide. • Set star nailhead above picture. • Glue stand on.

BABIES PLAY
by Renée Plains
MATERIALS: *Design Originals Legacy Papers* (#0495 Brown floral, #0547 Dictionary) • Foam core • Small picture • Copper eyelets • Star nailhead • Tarnished copper foil tape • Adhesive
INSTRUCTIONS: Make frame. • Cover front with dictionary text. • Cut $1/4$" strips of floral paper. Glue strips around edge of frame. • Glue picture in center of frame. Glue eyelets in at each corner. Set star nailhead above picture. • Glue stand on.

Timeless Cigar Box Purse
by Pam Hammons

MATERIALS: *Design Originals Legacy Papers* (#0492 Coffee floral, #0501 TeaDye clocks, 0499 TeaDye music, #0500 TeaDye keys) • *Design Originals Heritage Papers* (#0418 Love letters, #0410 Seasonal Postcards, #0411 Letter Postcards) • Cigar box • 16 gauge wire • Beads • Brass charms • *Lumiere* paints (Olive & Copper) • $1^1/_2$" Wooden plug • Fibers

INSTRUCTIONS: Drill $^1/_8$" holes for latch in the center of front side of box and holes for handle $2^1/_2$" on either side of center. • Paint sides and edges of cigar box with paints. • Cut paper into separate postcards and glue around all sides of the box in a zig zag pattern. • Trim off excess. • Cut paper to size and glue to top and bottom of cigar box. Tear and glue paper to top of box. • Then apply paper on top of other papers. • Repeat on bottom of box using paper. • On bottom of box tear and glue paper in two corners. • Cut paper into postcards and decorate top and bottom with several postcards. • Glue clock face to top of box and embellish with beads. • Glue on brass frame with green paper underneath to top of box. • Glue brass keys and hand charms to bottom. • Embellish post cards with beads. • Apply collage sealer to entire box. • Cut wire in a 10" length. • String beads. • Insert wire ends into holes; twist to secure. • Glue wooden plug and fibers to purse for closure. • Measure inside of box. • Cut and glue paper to inside of box.

Travels Cigar Box Purse
by Pam Hammons

MATERIALS: *Design Originals Legacy Paper* #0480 Green floral • *Design Originals Heritage Papers* (#0418 Love Letters, #0411 Letter Postcards) • Cigar box • 16 gauge wire • Beads • Brass charms • *Hero Arts* rubber stamps • Clay pieces • Tags • Fibers • *Cat's Eyes* Cocoa ink pad • *Lumiere* paints (Olive & Gold).

INSTRUCTIONS: Drill $^1/_8$" holes for latch in the center of front side of box and holes for handle $2^1/_2$" on either side of center. • Paint sides of box with Lumiere paints. • Cut paper to size and glue to top and bottom of box. • Tear paper in the shape of a country and glue to top of box. • Tear paper and glue on bottom of box. • Wipe Cat's Eyes Cocoa on edges to shade and antique. • Stamp on box • Glue on charms, beads and clay shapes. • Color tags and add fibers. • Attach to box. • Apply collage sealer. • Cut wire in a 10" length. • String beads. • Insert wire ends into holes and twist to secure. • Measure inside of box. • Cut and glue paper to inside of box.

Cigar Box Purses

Keep your favorite memories with you every day by decorating an easy purse.

Dress up your purse with a beaded handle and a wooden knob for closure.

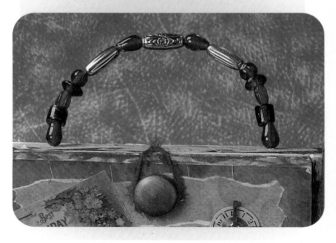

Use Mega Punches
to Create Classy Pages

Make decorating your pages quick and easy by using Mega punch shapes for quick decoration with *Legacy* papers.

Legacy Papers' coordinated colors and patterns make creating pages so much fun! Everything looks great, no matter what you choose!

FOUR SQUARES QUILT
by Shelley Petty

MATERIALS: *Design Originals Legacy Papers* (#0486 Blue floral, #0485 Blue stripe, #0484 Blue linen, #0490 Coffee linen, #0509 Butterfly Cuts, #0503 Scroll Frame) • 8 Copper eyelets • 4 Green eyelets • Fiber • Acid-free adhesive • Sewing machine

INSTRUCTIONS: Use a 12" x 12" floral sheet for background. • Cut two 6" x 6" squares from striped paper and mount one in top right corner and one in bottom left corner. Sew, using zig zag stitch, down the center vertically and across the center horizontally. • Cut two 3½" squares from a solid paper and cut each square into 2 triangles. Place triangle in each outer corner of background sheet. Zig zag stitch along the inside edge of each triangle. • Tape all loose threads on the back of background sheet. Zig zag stitch around all four sides of background sheet. • Cut out four Butterfly Cuts and center in each corner triangle. Add eyelets to end of antennas on butterflies.

HALLOWEEN QUILT
by Shelley Petty

MATERIALS: *Design Originals Legacy Papers* (#0493 Brown linen, #0494 Brown stripe, #0495 Brown floral, #0506 Halloween Cuts) • Fibers • 16 Brads • Chevron punch • *Cat's Eye* Bronze ink pad • Orange and Tan paper • Chalk • Acid-free adhesive

INSTRUCTIONS: Cut two ½" x 12" strips from Brown striped paper. • Center the strip vertically and horizontally across the Tan background paper. • Punch out 16 chevrons. Age them by wrinkling them and inking direct to paper with a bronze Cat's Eye ink pad. Place in the corners formed by the 2 strips. • Cut four 4" squares out of dark solid paper. Center on point on background sheet in each square section. Place brad in each corner of 4" square and wrap and string fibers around them. • Attach a Pumpkin Cut in the center to cover the overlapped paper.

Make legacy books for holiday celebrations. Don't forget to add title pages!

LETTER QUILT
by Shelley Petty

MATERIALS: *Design Originals Legacy Papers* (#0490 Coffee linen, #0491 Coffee stripe, #0501 TeaDye clocks, #0497 TeaDye letters, #0493 Brown linen, #0495 Brown floral) • Black pen • Chevron punch • Fleur de lis punch • Acid-free adhesive

INSTRUCTIONS: Make a light mark at the center point on all four sides or TeaDye letters paper. • Cut a 4 1/2" square out of Brown floral paper and cut into two triangles. • Cut a 4" square out of Brown linen paper and cut into two triangles. • Place the center point of a floral triangle onto the pen mark you made at the top of the background sheet and one at the bottom of the sheet. Place the center point of a linen triangle onto the pen marks you made on the right and left side of the background sheet. • Cut a 4" square out of Brown linen paper and mat on point in center of background sheet. • Cut four strips of striped paper 1/4" x 7" and adhere strips to edges of triangles. Trim overlap off. • Punch eight chevrons out of Coffee linen paper and adhere to the eight corners of the center pieces. • Punch 4 Fleur de lis out of TeaDye clocks and adhere under the outside chevrons. • Cut two 4" squares of TeaDye clocks and tear each square from point to point to make triangles. Mount a triangle at each outer edge of the background sheet. • Punch 4 chevrons out of Coffee linen and adhere to each of the 4 outer corners. • Punch 4 Fleur de lis out TeaDye clocks and place one under each chevron. • Trace around all punch art with a black pen.

Crop your snapshots to focus on just your loved ones. Add Legacy borders and letters to embellish.

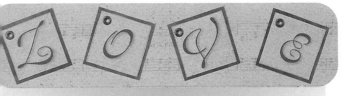

Attach *Legacy* Alphabet letters on your page with eyelets for elegant lettering.

LOVE
by Shelley Petty

MATERIALS: *Design Originals Legacy Papers* (#0490 Coffee linen, #0495 Brown floral, #0498 TeaDye tapestry, #0496 TeaDye alphabet, #0493 Brown linen, #0499 TeaDye music) • 12 Copper eyelets • Decorative punch • Acid-free adhesive

INSTRUCTIONS: Use Coffee linen for background sheet. Using Legacy Alphabet Sheet cut out the letters to spell 'LOVE'. Mat each letter on Brown linen paper. Cut out decorative swirl border from alphabet sheet into 1 1/4" x 12" strip and mat onto 1 1/2" x 12" strip of dark solid paper. Mount border to top of background sheet leaving 1/4" border at the top. Tear a 3" x 12" strip from TeaDye music paper and adhere to background sheet 2 inches from the top. Place the alphabet letters on top of this strip and attach with eyelets. Cut two 4 1/2" x 6" pieces from Brown floral paper and center and mount them at bottom of background sheet. Cut four 1 1/2" squares; cut each into 2 triangles and mount at corners of Brown floral mats. Punch out eight decorative shapes and mount on top of triangles with eyelets.

A scroll frame and decorative corners plus jewels and zig zag stitching make our Frame Quilt page truly unique.

Use *Legacy* Frames to highlight your most precious photos.

FRAME QUILT
by Shelley Petty

MATERIALS: *Design Originals Legacy Papers* (#0479 Green stripe, #0480 Green floral, #0498 TeaDye tapestry, #0503 Scroll Frame) • 4 Jewels • Pop Dots • Sewing machine • Acid-free adhesive

INSTRUCTIONS: Cut four 1" x 12" strips of striped paper. Adhere the strips to the background paper leaving a 1" border around the outside. Zig zag stitch down all sides of strips; tape the loose ends onto the back. • Cut an 8" square in floral paper and center on background paper on point. Stitch around outside of 8" square. • Cut out a Legacy Frame and center in the 8" square using pop dots for dimension. • Attach Legacy Corner to each point of square and glue a gem in each point.

GREEN CHRISTMAS QUILT
by Shelley Petty

MATERIALS: *Design Originals Legacy Papers* (#0479 Green stripe, #0480 Green floral, #0478 Green linen, #0504 Holiday Cuts) • Light solid paper • Chevron punch • Black pen • Sewing machine • Acid-free adhesive

INSTRUCTIONS: Cut two $^1/_2$" x 12" strips from dark striped paper. Center the strips vertically and horizontally across a floral background sheet. Zig zag along all four sides of these strips. • Zig zag stitch around the perimeter of the background sheet. • Cut four $4^3/_4$" squares from linen paper and center in each of the squares on background sheet. • Cut four $4^1/_4$" squares of light solid paper and mat on the $4^3/_4$" squares. • Cut two $4^1/_4$" squares of floral paper and cut each into two triangles. Place each triangle in outer corner of light squares. • Punch 16 chevrons out of linen paper and place in star format at the center of the squares. • Blanket stitch around outside of stars with a black pen. • Attach a Holiday Cut in center of the background sheet.

Quilt Lovers... create your legacy pages around a collection of your favorite quilt designs.

More Ideas for Punches

NAVY AND TEAL QUILT
by Shelley Petty

MATERIALS: *Design Originals Legacy Papers* (#0484 Blue linen, #0483 Teal floral, #0482 Teal stripe, #0498 TeaDye tapestry) • Fleur de lis punch • Diamond punch • 10 eyelets • Black pen • Acid-free adhesive

INSTRUCTIONS: Use 12" x 12" Teal floral paper as background sheet. • Tear two 1 1/2" x 12" Blue linen strips and glue vertically 1" in from outside edges. • Center 8" x 12" piece of TeaDye tapestry and glue on page. • Glue 1" x 12" Teal stripe paper to cover edges of TeaDye tapestry and Blue linen. • Center and glue two 4" squares of Blue linen on TeaDye tapestry. • Cut four 2" squares of Teal floral and cut each into 2 triangles. Glue triangles to corners of Blue linen squares. • Punch 8 Fleur de lis out of TeaDye tapestry and adhere to each triangle. • Punch ten diamonds out of Blue linen paper and center 5 vertically on both striped panels. • Add eyelets to the center of each diamond. • Trace around the outside of all punched shapes with a black pen.

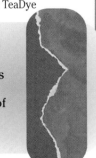

Create great borders with strips of torn paper.

TEAL CHRISTMAS QUILT
by Shelley Petty

MATERIALS: *Design Originals Legacy Papers* (#0483 Teal floral, #0482 Teal stripe, #0481 Teal linen, #0497 TeaDye letters, #0504 Holiday Cuts) • Tan cardstock • Chevron punch • Black pen • Acid-free adhesive • Tape • Fibers • Eyelets

INSTRUCTIONS: Tear a 2" x 12" strip out of letters paper and adhere to the right edge of background sheet about 1" in. • Cut a 6 1/4" x 12" piece of Tan cardstock. • Cut a 6" x 12" piece of Teal stripe paper. Center it on the Tan cardstock. • Cut two 5 1/2" squares of Teal floral paper and center on striped paper. Cut 4" squares of Teal linen and glue in the center of the 5 1/2" squares. • Punch 8 chevrons out of Tan cardstock. Adhere one to each corner of 4" square. Add blanket stitch around edges of chevrons with a black pen. • Adhere the whole panel to the left side of the pages, leaving 2" of border paper. • Make two small notches in top of paper and two in bottom of paper about 1/4" from panel edges to secure fiber. • String fiber and tape end on the back.

BLUE FLOWER QUILT
by Shelley Petty

MATERIALS: *Design Originals Legacy Papers* (#0486 Blue floral, #0484 Blue linen, #0485 Blue stripe, #0508 Floral Cuts) • Dark Blue cardstock 1 1/2" Square scallop punch • 1/2" Blue ribbon • Chalk • Sewing machine • Acid-free adhesive

INSTRUCTIONS: Cut a 3" x 12" strip of striped paper with the stripes running in the 3" direction. Mount it to the bottom of a 12" x 12" solid Blue background sheet. • Cut a 1/2" x 12" strip out of the striped paper wit • Cut three 7" squares out of floral paper. Cut each square into 2 triangles and place on page. Zig zag stitch around triangles. Do not stitch outside edges. • Cut two ovals 5" x 4 1/8" and mount them in center of dark solid spaces. Zig zag stitch around outside of ovals. • Place ribbon across the bottom of the page. Center it from top to bottom between the 3" strip. • Punch 5 scalloped 1 1/2" squares. Put Floral Cuts on top. Chalk around edges. Glue these squares on point along the ribbon.

Paper Mache Boxes

by Renée Plains

INSTRUCTIONS: Measure box and cut strips slightly larger than measurement so that it can be trimmed after it is glued on box. Cutting strips allows for covering larger areas, for instance, around the box. For square or rectangle boxes, start by laying paper on at a corner. • Paint PVA glue on one side of a smaller box, or on a round box paint about 4" to 5". Lay the paper on the glue lining up as many of the paper edges with the box edges as possible so that fewer sides will need to be trimmed. Use a brayer to smooth the paper on the box. Paint PVA on the next side or section and lay the paper over this glued section using a brayer to continue smoothing. Trim paper that extends beyond edge with scissors or an X-Acto knife. Continue until all sides of box are covered. • Add trim strips using decorative paper scissors and PVA glue or a glue stick. Use brown decorating chalk on the white edges that show from cutting the paper.

Flatten an old bottle cap to use as a tiny frame. Place a charm or a small photo inside.

COFFEE FLORAL BOX
by Renée Plains

MATERIALS: *Design Originals Legacy Papers* (#0492 Coffee floral, #0491 Coffee stripe) • Medium paper maché box • Small antique round brads • Small picture • *Books by Hand* PVA adhesive

INSTRUCTIONS: Cover box with paper. • Cut 5/8" strips from stripe paper. Trim one edge with decorative paper scissors. Glue straight edge along lid edge. • Glue small picture to box lid. Cut 1/4" strips from stripe paper. Make a frame around picture with these strips. Put small brads at each corner of picture.

1922 JOURNEY BOX
by Renée Plains

MATERIALS: *Design Originals Legacy Papers* (#0498 TeaDye tapestry, #0492 Coffee floral) • Small round paper maché box • Small picture • Rubber stamps (*Zettiology* label; *Limited Edition* #8531H script) • Embroidery floss • Tan text weight paper • *Books by Hand* PVA adhesive

INSTRUCTIONS: Cover box with paper. • Stamp script stamp and label stamps on tan paper. Write 1922 in small label and 'journey' in other label. Cut a square from script stamp and glue to lid. Cut out labels and glue on box. Chalk edges to age paper. • Cut out a square from floral paper with small scallop decorative paper scissors to make frame. Cut a picture slightly smaller and glue to frame. Sew a small cross stitch to each corner of picture and glue to script square on box.

PENCIL CUP
by Renée Plains

MATERIALS: *Design Originals Legacy Papers* (#0486 Blue floral, #0497 TeaDye letters, #0494 Brown stripe) • Tin can • Rubber stamps (*Limited Edition* #8776L Pen nib; *Zettiology* Label; Numbers) • *Books by Hand* PVA

INSTRUCTIONS: Remove label from can and any lumpy glue. Measure and cut paper strip to go around can. Apply adhesive with Xyron to paper and put paper on can. • Stamp pen nib stamp on letters paper and cut out. Cut a piece of stripe paper slightly larger than stamped paper for a border. Glue stamped paper to stripe paper, then to the can. • Cut a 1/4" strip of stripe paper and glue around bottom edge of cup. • Stamp label on paper. Stamp number inside label. Cut out label and glue on can.

NO. 95223 BOX
by Renée Plains

MATERIALS: *Design Originals Legacy Paper* #0500 TeaDye Keys • Paper maché box • Bottle cap • Rubber stamps (*Zettiology* label; *Limited Edition* #8531H script) • Diamond Glaze • Number stamp • Small picture • PVA

INSTRUCTIONS: Cover box with paper. • Flatten bottle cap with a rubber mallet by tapping it from the top of the bottle cap on a stack of newspapers until the edges flare/curl towards the top. Cut a circle with a large circle punch from paper and stamp script on the circle. Glue to the center of the bottle cap. Use a smaller circle punch to cut a picture to fit inside and glue in place. Use Diamond Glaze to coat pictures. When dry glue bottle cap to the top of box. • Stamp label on cream paper with brown ink. Stamp a number inside the label. Cut out label and chalk the edges to age. Glue under bottle cap.

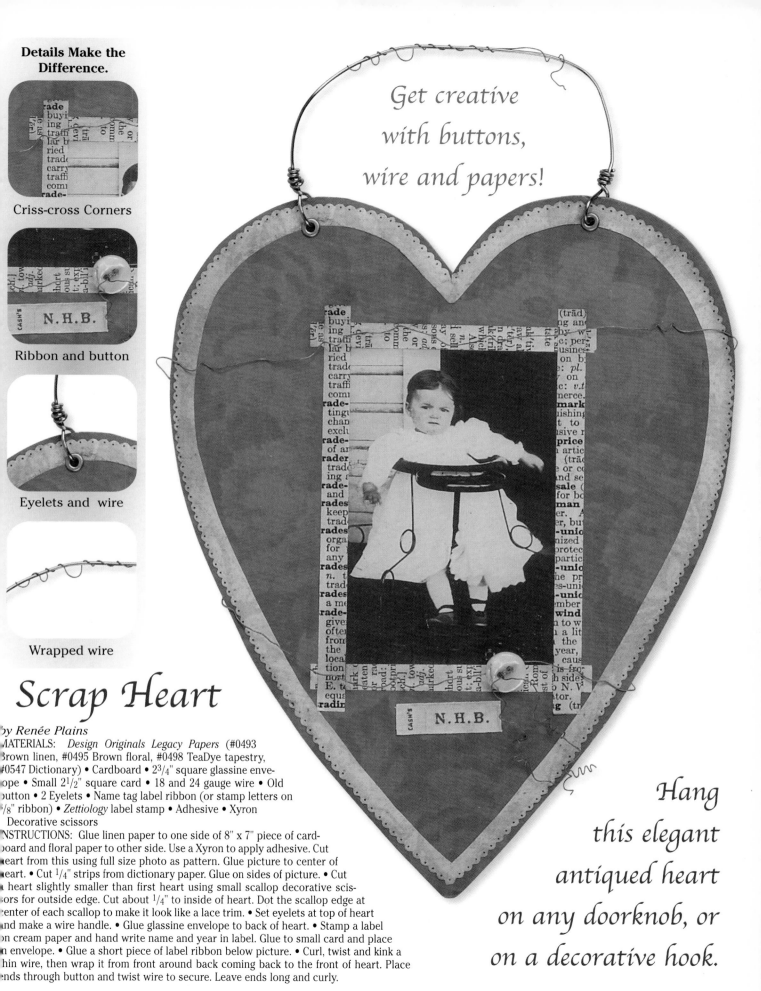

Details Make the Difference.

Criss-cross Corners

Ribbon and button

Eyelets and wire

Wrapped wire

Get creative with buttons, wire and papers!

Scrap Heart

by Renée Plains

MATERIALS: *Design Originals Legacy Papers* (#0493 Brown linen, #0495 Brown floral, #0498 TeaDye tapestry, #0547 Dictionary) • Cardboard • $2^3/4$" square glassine envelope • Small $2^1/2$" square card • 18 and 24 gauge wire • Old button • 2 Eyelets • Name tag label ribbon (or stamp letters on $^1/8$" ribbon) • *Zettiology* label stamp • Adhesive • Xyron • Decorative scissors

INSTRUCTIONS: Glue linen paper to one side of 8" x 7" piece of cardboard and floral paper to other side. Use a Xyron to apply adhesive. Cut heart from this using full size photo as pattern. Glue picture to center of heart. • Cut $^1/4$" strips from dictionary paper. Glue on sides of picture. • Cut a heart slightly smaller than first heart using small scallop decorative scissors for outside edge. Cut about $^1/4$" to inside of heart. Dot the scallop edge at center of each scallop to make it look like a lace trim. • Set eyelets at top of heart and make a wire handle. • Glue glassine envelope to back of heart. • Stamp a label on cream paper and hand write name and year in label. Glue to small card and place in envelope. • Glue a short piece of label ribbon below picture. • Curl, twist and kink a thin wire, then wrap it from front around back coming back to the front of heart. Place ends through button and twist wire to secure. Leave ends long and curly.

Hang this elegant antiqued heart on any doorknob, or on a decorative hook.

Wrap twine to link paper collage boxes together.

DEER HUNTING
by Laura Gregory

MATERIALS: *Design Originals Legacy Papers* (#0493 Brown linen, #0494 Brown stripe, #0500 TeaDye keys) • Hemp • *Bazzill* cardstock • Jute • *Stop N Crop* netting • Eyelets • *American Tag* tag

INSTRUCTIONS:
Tear a 1½" strip from edge of paper. Then tear another 1" strip next to that and discard. • Adhere netting to 2" x 12" Tan cardstock. Glue strip to the top strip and the main paper. • Glue torn pieces of paper to tag to create a 'camo' effect. • Set an eyelet in the tag and thread jute through the hole. • Make 5 'camo' squares. Cover the squares with netting and glue on the page. Wrap hemp around the squares.

Making beautiful pages with your pictures assures your photographic legacy as part of the past, present and future.

Our Legacy Memories Book was designed to help energize your creativity!

Embellish pages with metal frames to make your journaling stand out.

MY SWEET NICOLE
by Laura Gregory

MATERIALS: *Design Originals Legacy Papers* (#0488 Rust stripe, #0487 Rust linen, #0490 Coffee linen) • Natural colored paper • Green paper • Gold paper • *7 gypsies* Metal frames and metal corners • Acid-free adhesive • Pop Dots

INSTRUCTIONS:
Tear a 3" Green strip and glue down on left edge of background paper. • Place journaling in the metal frames and then add brads in the holes of the frames. Glue frames on the page. • Double mat the poem and mount it on the page with Pop Dots. • Glue the brass photo corners on the page.

Rustic Pages

Add small brads and nailheads to give a rustic look.

COWBOY

by Renée Plains

MATERIALS: *Design Originals Legacy Papers* (#0493 Brown linen, #0490 Coffee linen, #0487 Rust linen) • Die-cut letters • Star nailheads • *NRN Designs* Stickers

INSTRUCTIONS: Use Brown linen paper for the background sheet. • Cut a 12" x 3½" piece of Coffee linen paper and adhere to bottom of page. • Cut out three 5½" x 2½" photos and adhere to left side of page. • Cut out a 2" x 4¾" photo and adhere to right side of page. • Place stickers around photo to form a frame. • Cut one 3" square and three ¾" squares out of Rust linen paper for journaling. Adhere to page with acid-free adhesive. • Adhere die-cut letters to page for title. • Place star nailheads on each side of title. • Journal by each photo with a Black pen.

Rubber stamp images directly onto *Legacy* papers for a great look.

REMEMBER THE PAST

by Renée Plains

MATERIALS: *Design Originals Legacy Papers* (#0488 Rust stripe, #0487 Rust linen) • *Rubbermoon* stamped images • *Rubbermoon* word stamps • Brown ink • *Me & My Big Ideas* stickers

INSTRUCTIONS: Use striped paper for the background sheet • Tear a 12" x 1½" piece of linen paper. • Stamp images and words with brown ink on strip. • Adhere 1½" from bottom of page. • Adhere three photos on page. • Place stickers around photos to form frames • Print title and journaling on linen paper and cut out. • Adhere to page with acid-free adhesive.

Decorate Fabulous Frames with Papers and Details!

WOODEN FRAMES
by Renée Plains

INSTRUCTIONS: Paint wooden frame with gesso or wood sealer. • Paint inside edges and about 1/2" of top inside edge with dark brown paint. This will allow for less precision if covering edge with paper or it can be left as is. • Cut paper slightly larger than frame. Paint PVA glue on frame top. Lay paper on frame and smooth with a brayer. • Lay frame with the front down and cut an "X" from inside corners using a sharp X-Acto knife. Cut along inside edges with X-Acto knife and remove paper. Trim outside edges following along edge. • Cut enough strips of paper to glue around outer edge of frame. Glue strips on frame with PVA glue. Use brayer to smooth paper.

Tarnish copper mesh with Liver of Sulphur.

TRACK TEAM PICTURE FRAME

MATERIALS: *Design Originals Legacy Paper* #0483 Teal floral • Wooden frame • Color print of rust colored ruler • *AMACO* #50080H 80 wire mesh woven copper • *RIO Grande* Liver of Sulphur • Star nailhead • *7 gypsies* script scrapbook paper • Copy of an old sepia tone photo • *Books by Hand* PVA adhesive • Glue Dots

INSTRUCTIONS: Cover frame with paper. • Cut a 1/4" strip of decorative edge paper. Glue in place along inside edge with glue stick. • Tear a 1" x 1 1/4" rectangle from 80 wire mesh woven copper that has been tarnished with Liver of Sulphur. Place star nailhead on rectangle pushing points to the back and fold back points to secure. Adhere to the center top of the frame with Glue Dots. • Cut a piece of script paper and a piece of cardboard to fit frame opening. Glue script paper to cardboard. • Trim photo with deckle decorative paper scissors. Glue photo on script paper and put in frame.

Add chalking to victorian sticker labels to create a beautiful heritage look.

SWEET CHERRIES FRAME

MATERIALS: *Design Originals Legacy Papers* (#0495 Brown floral, #0498 TeaDye tapestry) • Wooden frame • *ARTchix Studio* #C202 Karen's Faves collage sheet 'Girl with Cherries' picture • Rubber stamps (*A Stamp in the Hand* script; *Limited Edition* #JV186E script; *Postmodern Design* #VT1-106D 'Remember') • Liver of Sulphur • *AMACO* medium copper • *Mrs. Grossman's* label sticker • *Books by Hand* PVA adhesive • Glue Dots • *CrafT Products* chalk

INSTRUCTIONS: Cover frame with paper. • Stamp 'Remember' on label. Use brown and black chalk on edges to age if desired. • Place sticker on frame at center under opening. • Stamp small script stamp on tapestry paper. Tear paper around stamp leaving about an 1/8" border. Chalk edges to age. Glue to center top above opening in frame. • Punch small heart from copper that has been tarnished with Liver of Sulphur. Adhere heart at center of script with Glue Dots. • Cut a piece of tapestry paper and a piece of cardboard to fit frame opening. Stamp large script stamp on paper and glue to cardboard. • Trim girl with cherries collage sheet picture with small scallop decorative paper scissors. Glue photo on the script paper and put in frame.

Paper Mache Ornaments Look Charming on Christmas Trees and They Make Welcome Gifts!

PAPER MACHÉ ORNAMENTS *by Renée Plains*

INSTRUCTIONS: Cut two pieces of paper just slightly larger than the ornament. • Paint PVA glue on one side and lay the paper on the glue smoothing with a brayer. • Trim the excess paper with scissors or an X-acto knife. Repeat for back of ornament. • Cut 3/8" strips of paper and glue to edges of ornament. Use brown decorating chalks to cover the white edges of cut paper.

Pewter nailheads, brads, frames, charms and letters are a perfect match with *Legacy* papers.

Add a few of Grandmother's buttons to personalize your page, frame or ornament.

Frame a photo in a small slide mount covered with *Legacy* decorative paper.

CHRISTMAS   *by Renée Plains*

MATERIALS: *Design Originals Legacy Paper* #0480 Green floral • Paper Maché Ornament • Zig .005 Millennium black pen • Star nailhead • *Zettiology* label stamp • *CraftT Products* chalk • Picture of angel • Adhesive

INSTRUCTIONS: Cover ornament with floral paper. • Cut picture with small scallop decorative paper scissors. Glue picture to ornament. • Stamp label on green paper. Write Christmas in label with ZIG pen. Chalk edges of label with brown and black chalk. Glue below picture. • Set star nailhead above angel picture.

1912   *by Renée Plains*

MATERIALS: *Design Originals Legacy Papers* (#0492 Coffee floral, #0491 Coffee stripe, #0498 TeaDye tapestry) • Paper Maché Ornament • Small picture of girl • Scrap of cream text weight paper • Zig .005 Millennium black pen • *CraftT Products* chalk • Three small buttons • Photo slide mount • Adhesive

INSTRUCTIONS: Cover ornament with floral, tapestry and stripe paper. • Cover a slide mount with stripe paper. Glue picture and mount to ornament. • Write 1912 on the text weight paper. Chalk edges with brown and black chalk. Glue above picture. • Glue buttons under picture.

OLIVIA   *by Renée Plains*

MATERIALS: *Design Originals Legacy Papers* (#0486 Blue floral, #0497 TeaDye letters, #0547 Dictionary) • Paper Maché Ornament • Zig .005 Millennium black pen • Heart charm • *Zettiology* label stamp • Picture of little girl • Photo slide mount • *CraftT Products* chalk • Adhesive

INSTRUCTIONS: Cover ornament with floral paper. • Cover a slide mount with letters paper. • Tear a square of dictionary paper and glue to ornament. Glue picture and frame to dictionary square. • Stamp label on paper. Write Olivia in label. Chalk edges of label with brown and black chalk. Glue below picture. • Glue heart charm above picture.

Use cardstock and floss to create a hanging picture for your page.

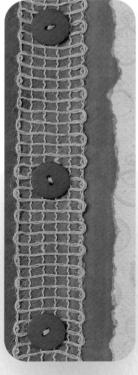

Add interest to your page with eyelets. Thread textured fibers through the eyelets and tie in a bow.

Chalk around the edges of blocks to give a vintage look.

Add special details with a strip of mesh, a strip of torn paper and buttons.

OUR TIME TOGETHER

by Christy Lemond

MATERIALS: *Design Originals Legacy Papers* (#0501 TeaDye clocks, #0495 Brown floral, #0485 Blue stripe) • *Bazzill* cardstock • *Stop N Crop* fiber and netting • *Creative Imagination* large eyelets • *CrafT Products* chalk • *Making Memories* buttons • *DMC* floss • Acid-free adhesive • Glue Dots

INSTRUCTIONS: Tear a 2 1/2" Blue stripe border and glue to background paper. Glue netting to this border. Thread each button with DMC floss and attach to netting with Glue Dots. • Tear a square and thread with DMC floss for the title block. Chalk around the title block for an aged look. • Chalk edges around the entire page. Print the poem on cardstock. Tear and chalk the edges of the poem. • Set eyelets on the side and thread fibers through the holes, tying them in a bow. • To create the button bar between the photos, thread each button with DMC floss and then glue them to the page using Glue Dots. • Chalk edges around the entire page.

Just for fun! Take a black slide mount and turn it into a tiny 'shaker'.

KEY TO MY HEART
by Laura Gregory

MATERIALS: *Design Originals Legacy Papers* (#0500 TeaDye keys, #0496 TeaDye alphabet, #0501 TeaDye clocks, #0499 TeaDye music, #0497 TeaDye letters) • *Bazzill* cardstock • *Z Barten* confetti • *Jest Charming* key charm • *Jest Charming* black slide mount • Heart brad • Eyelets • Acid-free adhesive • Pop Dots

INSTRUCTIONS: Take an 7¼" x 9¼" solid black cardstock and glue pieces of torn paper all over to create a collage background effect. • Mat your photo twice and adhere to the collage background. • To create the side banner, print title on 3" x 9" cardstock. Set eyelets in each corner and thread DMC floss through the holes and attach them to the page with heart brads. • To make the shaker in the middle, take a slide mount and glue a clear piece of plastic over the opening. Add two layers of foam tape around the edges of the slide mount. Pour shaker contents inside the box you've created. Place another sheet of clear plastic to close the box. Adhere to your page.

Preserve your family memories with acid-free Legacy papers.

KEY TO FRIENDSHIP
by Christy Lemond

MATERIALS: *Design Originals Legacy Papers* (#0500 TeaDye keys, #0501 TeaDye clocks, #0492 Coffee floral, #0489 Rust floral • *Bazzill* cardstock • *Adornament* fibers • *Jest Charming* key charms • Acid-free adhesive • Pop Dots

INSTRUCTIONS: Tear a 3" strip of clocks paper and cut a 1" wide Brown floral strip. Glue the floral paper under the clocks paper to create a small edge. Glue this border to your page. • Take several kinds of fibers and twist them together. Included in the twisted fibers, take a strand of DMC floss and tie charms to it approx. 2" apart. • Double mat your photos and adhere them to the page. • Type your journaling on cardstock and then tear around the edges. Chalk the edges of the journal blocks to give the page added depth. Mount with Pop Dots.

BOYS IN A TREE
by Ruth Ann Warwick

MATERIALS: *Design Originals Legacy Papers* (#0499 TeaDye music, #0490 Coffee linen) • *DMC* floss • *Bazzill* cardstock • *Family Treasure* leaf buttons • Acid-free adhesive • Glue Dots

INSTRUCTIONS: Type journaling on computer. Cut each word out separately and mat them. • Mat each photo. • Thread each button with DMC floss and adhere to the page using Glue Dots.

Use foam Dots and flower pots to add a 3D look to your page.

AMY AND DADDY
by Delores Frantz

MATERIALS: *Design Originals Legacy Papers* (#0486 Blue floral, #0501 TeaDye clocks, #0493 Brown linen) • Cardstock (Red, Blue, Yellow, Rust, Pale Green) • Vellum • 18" of Blue $1/2$" flat braid • Pop Dots • *Sizzix* dies ($1^3/4$" flower and 1" leaf) • *Sizzix* die cutter • Acid-free adhesive

INSTRUCTIONS: Cover album page with clocks paper. • Cut photo into a silhouette and glue to center of page. • Cut side curtains and valance from floral paper, attach to page using Pop Dots. Glue braid to curtains. • Cut one 1" x 12" strip, four $1/4$" x 12" strips and three $3/4$" x 12" strips of paper. Glue strips together to form window. • Attach to page with Pop Dots. Some Dots will have to be stacked to keep window level. • Cut flower pots, flowers, leaves and stems from cardstock. Glue together, attach to window with Pop Dots. • Use computer to print words on vellum and attach to page.

Every memory is a precious legacy. The things you preserve for future generations become cherished possessions, and they are precious in the present as well.

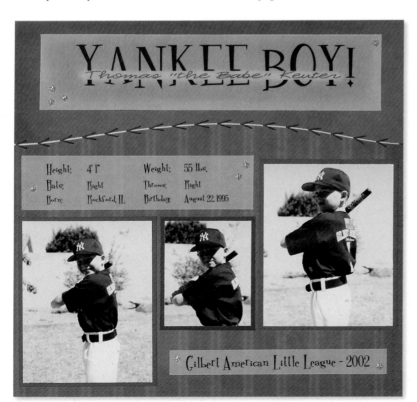

Create a fabulous title by printing on Vellum paper with your computer. Add color chalking for a great look.

Stitch a wavy border to your page.

YANKEE BOY
by Susan Keuter

MATERIALS: *Design Originals Legacy Papers* (#0485 Blue stripe, #0484 Blue linen) • *Bazzill* (Cardstock, Heavyweight Vellum) • *DMC* Floss • *Scrapbook Barn* Silver Star Nailheads • *Craf-T Products* Chalk • Acid-free adhesive

INSTRUCTIONS: Cut curved $3^1/2$" x 12" Blue linen header and glue to top of page. • With floss, stitch border. • Print title on $2^1/2$" x $10^1/2$" vellum and chalk. Print on $1^3/4$" x 7" and $3/4$" x $6^1/2$" vellum. • Mat photos with cardstock and adhere to page. • Attach vellum strips with star nailheads.

Metal letter, tags, eyelets and charms add interest to any page.

A BAD HAIR DAY
by Tim Holtz

MATERIALS: *Design Originals Legacy Papers* (#0485 Blue stripe, #0484 Blue linen) • *Petersen Arne* card-stock (Dark Brown, Light Teal) • *Making Memories* Letter eyelets • Vellum tags • Mini brads • Snaps • *Toybox* crackle stamp • *Ranger* Black archival ink • *Postmodern* walnut ink • Scissor charm • Glue stick • Mounting tape • *Beacon* Kid's Choice glue • Sandpaper • Copy Paper

INSTRUCTIONS: Lightly sand stripe paper for background. • Randomly stamp crackle over page using Archival Ink. • Soak linen paper in walnut ink and let dry. • Mount photos onto cardstock. Tear linen paper to fit photos. Secure with snaps. • Spell out title with eyelets and secure letters with mini brads on linen paper. Mount onto cardstock. • Dye copy paper with walnut ink, crinkle up and let dry. • Print out journaling on dyed paper by lightly gluing it to a regular piece of paper and run through your printer. • Mount photos, titles, and journal to page using mounting tape. • Embellish page with vellum tags, charms and saved hair tied with ribbon.

Add pebbles to raffia to add depth and personality to your page.

ASHLEY AT BIG LAKE

by Carol Wingert

MATERIALS: *Design Originals Legacy Paper* #0486 Blue floral paper • *7 gypsies* Glass bottle • *7 gypsies* walnut ink • *Suze Weinberg* ultra thick embossing enamel • *Ranger* embossing ink and stippling ink • *Memory Lane* bookboard frame • *Anima Designs* barkskin paper • Raffia • Pebbles • *Hero Arts* alphabet stamps • Acid-free adhesive

INSTRUCTIONS: Tear papers into strips, adhere to a tan piece of cardstock to resemble small waves. • Randomly cover surface with clear embossing ink and clear UTEE. Heat until melted. • Stipple and sponge remaining cardstock with sepia ink. • Crumple small tag, age with walnut ink. Use for journaling or a title. • Fill small bottle with clean sand. • On piece of barkskin paper, arrange photo, small framed photo and pebbles. Adhere. Sew raffia over pebbles to secure. • Hang tag and small bottle from pebble. • Stamp title on the frame.

Preserve Your Memories with Legacy Papers and Details!

Weave strips of paper for a
terrific page border.

Cut out butterflies to
add to the border.

Use black buttons
and stickers for titles.

Add
stitches for details.

CLASS PHOTO
by Laura Gregory

MATERIALS: *Design Originals Legacy Papers* (#0486 Blue floral, #0485 Blue stripe, #0509 Butterfly Cuts) • *Bazzill* cardstock • Acid-free adhesive

INSTRUCTIONS: Cut three strips of patterned paper and mount on ivory cardstock. • On the left edge of your background paper cut $3^{1}/_{4}$" slits every 1". • Weave the patterned strips along the end of the background paper and slide photo tab adhesive at the top and bottom of each strip. • Cut out Butterfly Cuts and adhere to page above and below the photo.

MOTHER'S DAY
by Laura Gregory

MATERIALS: *Design Originals Legacy Paper* #0486 Blue floral • *Bazzill* cardstock • *Scrapbook Borders* graffiti stickers • *Mark Enterprises* Class A peel stickers • Black buttons • Acid-free adhesive • Glue Dots

INSTRUCTIONS: To create the border, tear a strip of cardstock $1^{1}/_{2}$" x 12". With a piercing tool, pierce paper and sew DMC floss in X configurations along the torn edge of the border. • Double mat photo with cardstock, leaving a larger edge on the bottom and tear this edge. Pierce holes in the matting below the photo and stitch. • Type journaling on vellum. • Place sticker numbers on black buttons and attach buttons on the journal block with glue dots and at the same time adhere the vellum to the journal block with glue dots. • Pierce the paper of the journal block and then stitch.

Use *Legacy* 'cuts' and wound fibers to make
quick cards for every occasion.

CHRISTMAS CARD
by Shannon Smith

MATERIALS: *Design Originals Legacy Papers* (#0478 Green linen, #0505 Santa Cuts) • 5x7 card • *Judikins* Diamond Glaze • *The Papercut* Gold paper • *Adornaments* fibers • *Tombow* paper glue • Pop Dots • Craft knife • Paint brush • Ruler • *Fiskars* Paper Trimmers

INSTRUCTIONS: Trim paper to $9^{1}/_{2}$" x $6^{1}/_{2}$" and glue to inside of the card. Make sure to start at the fold in the center and smooth the paper to the outside edges, leaving a $1/_{4}$" border all the way around. • On the inside of the card, use a ruler and craft knife to make two slits in the center of the card 1" apart. Start $1^{1}/_{2}$" above the fold and continue to $1/_{4}$" below the fold. • Pull slit tab at fold in and fold the card in half making creases at the bottom and the top of the tab. Adhere photo to the tab, making sure that when the card is folded shut it does not stick out of the card. • Decorate the inside of the card with a message and Holiday Cuts. • Cut gold cardstock to $9^{1}/_{2}$" x $6^{1}/_{2}$", crease in center and glue to the outside of the card. This will cover up the hole made from the slit on the inside. • Trim a scrap piece of paper to fit in the center of the card atop the gold. • Wrap the top of the card in fiber, making sure to go behind the picture on the inside. • Cut out Holiday Cut and paint with Diamond Glaze. • Place on card with Pop Dots on the back.

Classy Cards & Greetings

Pewter frames, charms, hinges, alphabet letters, brads, eyelets and nail-heads look sensational with *Legacy* papers.

BIRTHDAY GREETINGS CARD
by Carol Wingert

MATERIALS: *Design Originals Legacy Paper* #0483 Teal floral • *Design Originals Heritage Paper* #0410 Seasonal Postcards • *7 gypsies* walnut ink • Ivory cardstock • *Plaid* paint and crackling medium • Adhesive

INSTRUCTIONS: Create a 4^1/$_2$" x 6^1/$_2$" card out of ivory cardstock. • Cut a 4" x 6" panel out of ivory cardstock • Cut 4 panels, each 2" x 3", 2 out of Teal floral paper and 2 out of ivory cardstock. • On the small ivory panels, paint with acrylic paint which coordinates with floral paper. When dry, apply crackle medium. After medium is dry, paint with ivory paint. When top coat is completely dry, paint surface with walnut ink to age. Allow to thoroughly dry. • Adhere decorative panels and aged wood panels to the ivory cardstock panel. Machine stitch a zig-zag stitch to connect the four rectangles. Using foam tape, adhere mini Victorian card to the center of the rectangles. • Adhere panel to face of card.

THANK YOU CARD
by Carol Wingert

MATERIALS: *Design Originals Legacy Papers* (#0495 Brown floral, #0490 Coffee linen) • Black cardstock • *7 gypsies* Black nailheads • *Inkadinkado/Dawn Houser* stamps • *Impress* rubber stamps • *Beads by Pamela* beads • *Ancient Page by Clearsnap* stamping and stippling ink • *Krylon* Gold leaf pen • Adhesive

INSTRUCTIONS: Stamp "frame" stamp onto linen paper. Stamp sentiment inside of frame. Stipple lightly around the inside area. • Glue beads on four sides and string beading wire through beads and around the four edges of the frame. • Adhere to a piece of black cardstock and cut around the frame, leaving a rim of black for contrast. Use a gold leaf pen around the edges of the black cardstock. • Using decorative edge scissors, cut floral paper into a 5" square. Stipple edges with black ink. • Adhere frame to floral panel and then to a 5^1/$_2$" square card. Insert black nail heads into the four corners. • Edge the black card with a gold leaf pen.

BOTANICAL FRAME CARD
by Carol Wingert

MATERIALS: *Design Originals Legacy Papers* (#0490 Coffee linen, #0502 Oval Frame) • *Craf-T Products* chalks • *Beads by Pamela* beads • *Pressed Petals* dried flowers • Adhesive

INSTRUCTIONS: Trim frame and round corners. • Age frame with soft tan and brown chalks. • Arranged pressed dried flowers in the oval area. • Glue beads into corners of frame. • Adhere to Coffee linen paper. • Adhere to face of card.

Eyelets, brads & snaps... the perfect companions to paper borders.

BON VOYAGE CARD
by Carol Wingert

MATERIALS: *Design Originals Legacy Papers* (#0490 Coffee linen, #0491 Coffee stripe) • *Design Originals Heritage Paper* #0412 Travel Postcards • Brass corners • Snaps • Stamps • Ink • Fibers • Adhesive

INSTRUCTIONS: • Make a library card pocket out of striped paper. Trim with coordinating solid paper and complete by adding snaps.
• Make a tag out of a coordinating cardstock. Adhere small postcards on the tag. • Using a masking technique, stamp travel related stamps around the postcards. • Punch a hole in the tag and add fibers.
• Cover a 5" x 7" piece of chipboard with fabric. • Add brass corners.
• Adhere to the face of a 5" x 7" card.

CHRISTMAS CARD instructions on page 42.

Create this fabulous Accordion book.

It folds up to fit safely in a metal CD box.

Decorate the box with Legacy paper to give a vintage look.

To finish the box, tie it with ribbon, then add a tag and an antique key.

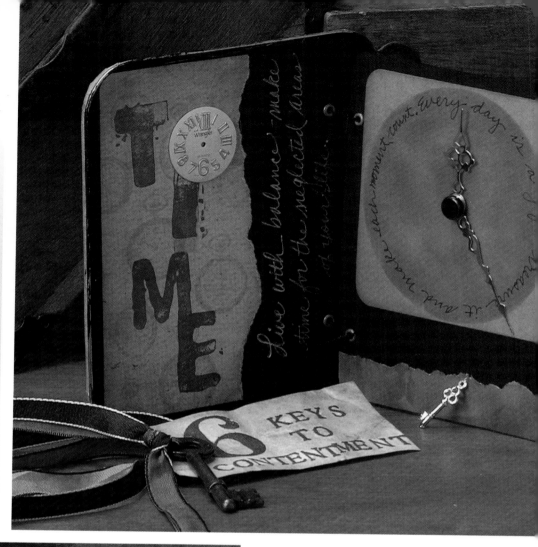

Accordion Book in a Box

TIN JOURNAL:
6 Keys to Contentment
by Carol Wingert

MATERIALS: *Design Originals Legacy Papers (#0500 TeaDye keys, #0501 TeaDye clocks, #0497 TeaDye letters, #0490 Coffee linen, #0492 Coffee floral)* • Aged tag • Spiral • Key charm • Watch face • *7 gypsies* Black nailheads • Rubber stamps *(Hero Arts, Magenta, Stampers Anonymous, Stampington & Co., Ma Vinci Reliquary, 100 Proof Press)*
• *Loose Ends* fiber paper • *Walnut Hollow* clock parts
• *Fancifuls* heart charm • *My Weakness* tree charm • *Golden* Black Gesso • *Plaid* Mod Podge • *Jacquard* neopaque paint
• Flat Tin- I used one which was mailed by an internet company to hold a CD • Adhesive • 40" of ³/₈" Ribbon
INSTRUCTIONS: Prepare tin by sanding first, then painting with black gesso. After gesso is dry, paint back of bottom tin with brown Neopaque paint. • Adhere key paper to lid with Mod Podge. When dry, apply several coats of Mod Podge to seal and protect cover. • Cut 6 panels out of black cardstock to fit inside tin. Round corners. • Add stamps, charms, tags and other collage elements on the face of each panel. Add journaling or word stamps. • Set eyelets in panels and tie together with waxed linen. The first and last panels will only have eyelets on one side. • Adhere the first panel to the inside of the tin cover and the last panel to the inside of the tin back. • Tie ribbons around the tin. Stamp a tag and add a key to the ribbon.

Apply gel to cardstock. Place image face down. Immediately rub across the image with a plastic spoon.

Pull up the original image by one corner. The image magically transfers to the cardstock. Chalk the edges.

Transfer Card
by Pam Hammons

MATERIALS: *Design Originals Legacy Paper* #0489 Rust floral • 8^1/$_2$" x 11" Beige cardstock • *Golden* regular matte gel medium • InkJet print for transfer • Clip art image • Glue stick • Deckle scissors • Plastic spoon • Q-tip

INSTRUCTIONS: Cut and fold beige cardstock into a 4^1/$_4$" x 7^1/$_2$" piece to make a card • Trim remaining cardstock into a 3^1/$_4$" x 6^1/$_2$" piece • With deckle scissors cut paper into a 3^3/$_4$" x 7" piece • Glue deckle cut paper to front of card • For transfer, copy the image desired onto 24# white copy paper using an water soluble Inkjet printer • Spread a small amount of gel medium onto the lower half of the 3^1/$_4$" x 6^1/$_2$" piece of cardstock where the image will be placed
• Carefully place transfer face down on gel medium
• Quickly and firmly rub the back of the transfer using the back of a plastic spoon. Peel up. Transferred image should remain. It will be slightly imperfect • With a Q-tip, rub brown chalk around image and edges of cardstock to give an antique look.

No matter how you what **love** spell it, this is looks like.

EMILY   JACE

Let young children tell stories and participate in making your pages. It's not just adults who have stories to share. Include everyday life with all its celebrations and happy occasions.

WHAT LOVE LOOKS LIKE
by Ruth Ann Warwick
MATERIALS: *Design Originals Legacy Papers* (#0493 Brown linen, #0497 TeaDye letters, #0496 TeaDye alphabet) • *Bazzill* cardstock • *C Thru Ruler* sticker letters • *Scrapbook Studio* rivets • Acid-free adhesive
INSTRUCTIONS: Cut six $1/4$" x 12" strips of Brown paper. Adhere two of them across the top of page approx 2" from the top. • Type title on cardstock and mat it. • Cut it in half and adhere each piece to the edge of the page using eyelets. • Place sticker letters on cardstock and then cut around each letter to create the mat look for the name. • Mount the sticker letters on a $2^1/4$" x 12"inch strip of paper. • Glue $4^1/4$" x 12" strips above and below the strip.

AT THE FRONT DOOR   *by Laura Gregory*
MATERIALS: *Design Originals Legacy Papers* (#0491 Coffee stripe, #0490 Coffee linen, #0486 Blue floral, #0507 Shoe Cuts) • *DMC* floss • Eyelets • Acid-free adhesive
INSTRUCTIONS: Cut a 4" x 12" strip of Coffee linen and glue to the left side of background paper. • Cut out the Shoe Cuts and space evenly on the border. • Set eyelets on the far left of the border and thread DMC floss through holes and tie in a bow. • Mount photo with an extra inch at the bottom and tear it to create a ragged edge. • Type journaling on cardstock and mount on coordinating paper, tearing the top edge.

Make a mini-album each month or have several different albums in process at the same time.

Use twigs or other embellishments to add to the theme of your page.

JAMES AND BEAU
by Delores Frantz

MATERIALS: *Design Originals Legacy Papers* (#0493 Brown linen, #0490 Coffee linen, #0494 Brown stripe) • Pale Gold cardstock • 4" of jute cord • Pop Dots • Twigs • 1/8" circle punch • Acid-free adhesive

INSTRUCTIONS: Glue one striped paper to album page. • Cut second striped paper diagonally from corner to corner forming 4 triangles. Glue the 2 triangles from the sides of paper to the top and bottom of album page matching outside edges. • Mat photo on a square of Brown linen paper. • Cut a larger square of Coffee linen paper. • Stack and center photo and Gold square on page. • Attach each layer to the one below it with Pop Dots. • Arrange and glue twigs along one side of page. • Print words on rectangle of Gold cardstock. Punch 2 holes in top of rectangle. • Attach to twig with jute cord. Glue twig to page.

In life, be completely present. Spend time right now making a scrapbook, frames or mini books with your family and friends. The hours spent are part of the pleasure!

Spark up any page with special embellishments from *7 gypsies.*

Add eyelets, clasps, snaps and shrink plastic charms.

FALL WITH FAMILY
by Carol Wingert

MATERIALS: *Design Originals Legacy Papers* (#0492 Coffee floral, #0493 Brown linen, #0490 Coffee linen) • *7 gypsies* Gold clasp • Snaps • Eyelets • *Hero Arts* stamps (Leaf and Alphabet stamps) • *Ranger* aging ink • *Polyshrink by Lucky Squirrel* shrink plastic • *Crafters by Color Box* ink • Acid-free adhesive

INSTRUCTIONS: Stamp maple leaf on clear polyshrink. With a permanent marker, write meaningful words on the leaf. Dab Crafters ink on leaves with your finger. Cut out leaves and punch a hole in the top. Shrink per manufacturer's directions. • Tear patterned and coordinating paper to fit corners of a 12" x 12" piece of Coffee linen paper. • Set 3 eyelets on the inside edge of the top corner. • Using gold clasps, wire and jump rings, fasten charms to corner. • Adhere corner to cardstock and add snaps. • Create a small "book" out of designer papers. Add journaling insert - computer generated on vellum, eyelets and a leaf charm. • Create small title piece from torn cardstock. Stamp title, set 2 eyelets and wire to cardstock. • Lay out and adhere photos, journaling "book" and remaining corner. Add snaps to corner.

How to Alter
Legacy Papers

In just minutes you can create fun variations of color and texture.

SANDED PAPER
Rub the surface of *Legacy* paper with a 100/220 grit sandpaper pad.

CRUMPLED PAPER
Crumple paper then flatten it, paint Walnut Ink over it to look like leather.

TORN PAPER
Pull paper toward you as you tear so a white edge will appear along the tear.

STAMP ON PAPER
Use a permanent ink pad and a rubber stamp design on *Legacy* paper.

Beautiful Borders

by Jennifer Maughan

REFLECT
MATERIALS: *Design Originals Legacy Papers* (#0493 Brown linen, #0496 TeaDye alphabet, #0499 TeaDye music) • *Design Originals Legacy Cuts* (#0507 Shoe Cuts) Black cardstock • Translucent Vellum • 2 *JewelCraft* Square dots

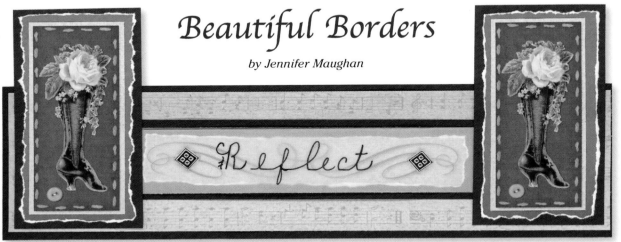

FLORAL
MATERIALS: *Design Originals Legacy Papers* (#0479 Green stripe, #0480 Green floral) • *Design Originals Legacy Cuts* (#0508 Floral Cuts) • Black cardstock • 2 *JewelCraft* Butterfly dots

DREAM
MATERIALS: *Design Originals Legacy Papers* (#0493 Brown linen, #0496 TeaDye alphabet, #0498 TeaDye tapestry) • Black cardstock

POSTCARDS
MATERIALS: *Design Originals Legacy Papers* (#0481 Teal linen, #0487 Rust linen, #0411 Letter Postcards, #0412 Travel Postcards) 3 Red buttons • 3 *JewelCraft* Longhorn dots

Weave a clever basket for Egg Hunting day... it's fun and easy!

EGG HUNTING
by Pam Hammons and Kristy McNeill

MATERIALS: *Design Originals Legacy Papers* (#0481 Teal linen, #0479 Green stripe, #0489 Rust floral, #0487 Rust linen, #0496 TeaDye alphabet) • 3 oval die-cuts for eggs

INSTRUCTIONS: Cut and weave the basket. Cut out the grass and alphabet squares. Assemble the page.

Weave a Basket

Legacy papers are perfect for paper weaving. Coordinated colors and patterns look great together. Weave a basket... try mixing different pattern combinations (floral, stripe and linen) on several different baskets to create a fabulous woven look!

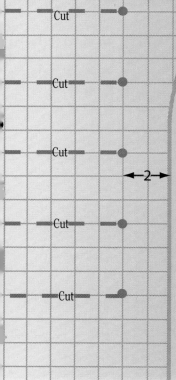

1. Copy and cut out pattern. Fold a piece of 6" x 6" *Legacy* paper in half. Line up the fold line then trace around the design.

2. Cut out basket design. Leave paper folded. Cut around design. Cut on grid lines as shown.

3. Weave paper. Cut 2 strips 1/8" (3 grids) wide. Weave one on each side of the basket.

4. Finish the handle. Cut 1 strip 1" (4 grids) wide. Weave in the center, cut a rounded top on the handle.

Suppliers: - Most craft and variety stores carry an excellent assortment of supplies. If you need something special, ask your local store to contact the following companies:

100 Proof Press, 740-594-2315, OH
7 gypsies, 480-325-3358, AZ
A Lost Art, 909-592-3067, CA
A Stamp In The Hand, 310-884-9700, CA
AccuCut Systems, 800-268-1670, NE
Acey Ducey, 518-398-5108, NY
Adornaments K1C2, 805-676-1176, CA
All Night Media, 678-291-8100, GA
American Tag, 800-223-3956, CA
Anima Designs, www.animadesigns.com
Art Accents, 360-733-8989, WA
ARTChix Studio, www.artchixstudio.com, Canada
Bazzill, 480-558-8557, AZ
Beacon Adhesives
Beads by Pamela, 480-821-2843, AZ
Books By Hand, 505-255-3534, NM
Boutique Trims, 248-437-2017, MI
Clearsnap, 800-448-4862, WA
Clipola/Cavallini Papers., 415-551-3590, CA
Colorbök, 800-366-4660, MI
Craf-T Products, 507-235-3996, MN
Creative Imaginations, 800-942-6487, CA
Creative Impressions, 719-577-4858, CO
C-Thru Ruler, 800-243-8419, CT
DCC, 316-685-6265, KS
Design Originals, 800-877-7820, TX www.d-originals.com
Diane Ribbon, 800-622-7263, AZ
DMC, 973-589-0606, NJ
DMD Industries, 800-805-9890, AR
Duncan, 800-237-2642, CA
E K Success, 800-524-1349, NJ
Emagination, 630-833-9521, IL
Embellish It!, 702-312-1628, NV
Family Treasures, 661-294-1330, CA
Fanciful, 607-849-6870, NY
Fiskars, 800-950-0203, WI
Glue Dots, 262-814-8500, WI
Golden Artist Colors, 800-959-6543, NY
Goodies from Grandma, 515-232-2423, IA
Green Pepper Press, www.greenpepperpress.com
Hero Art Stamps, 800-822-4376, CA
Impress Rubber Stamps, 206-901-9101, WA
Inkadinkadoo, 781-938-6100, MA
Jacquard, 800-442-0455, CA
Jesse James Button & Trim, 610-435-7899, PA
Jest Charming, 702-564-5101, NV
JewelCraft, 201-223-0804, NJ
Jolee's Boutique, 800-524-1349, NJ
JudiKins, 310-515-1115, CA
Karen Foster Designs, 801-451-9779, UT
Kolo, 860-547-0367, CT
Kreate-a-lope, 877-921-1015, NJ
Krylon, 800-457-9566, OH
Limited Edition, 650-299-9700, CA
Loose Ends, 503-390-7457, OR

Lucky Squirrel, 800-462-4912, NM
Ma Vinci's Reliquary, CO- www.crafts.dm.net/mall/reliquary
Magenta, 450-922-5253, Canada
Magic Mesh, 651-345-6374, MN
Making Memories, 801-294-0430, UT
Mark Enterprises, 800-869-0474, CA
Marvy Uchida, 800-541-5877, CA
Me & My Big Ideas, 949-589-4607, CA
Memory Lane, 480-844-9004, AZ
Mrs. Grossman's, 800-429-4549, CA
My Weakness, 480-632-6801, AZ
NRN Designs, 800-374-1600, IN
Offray, 908-879-4700, NJ
On The Surface, 847-675-2520, IL
Petersen-Arne, 909-817-5988, OR
Plaid Enterprises, 800-842-4197, GA
Pop Dots, 530-389-2233, CA
Postmodern Design, 405-321-3176, OK
Pressed Petals, 435-896-9531, UT
Printworks, 800-854-6558, CA
Provo Craft, 800-937-7686, UT
Ranger Industries, 800-244-2211, NJ
Rings & Things, 509-624-8565, WA
Rio Grande Jewelry, 800-545-6566, NM
Rubba-Dub-Dub, 707-748-0929, CA
Rubbermoon, 208-772-9772, ID
Scrapworks, 713-842-2547, TX
Scrapbook Barn, 480-503-2475, AZ
Scrapbook Borders, 850-651-7905, FL
Scrapbook Studios, 866-476-7380, MI
Sizzix, 800-253-2238, CA
Stampa Rosa, 800-554-5755, CA
Stampendous, 800-869-0474, CA
Stampers Anonymous, 440-250-9112, OH
Stampin' Up, 800-782-6787, UT
Stampington & Co., 949-380-7318, CA
Stanislaus, 800-227-4376, CA
Stop N Crop, www.stopncrop.com, TX
Suze Weinberg Studios, 732-761-2400, NJ
The Paper Cut, 920-954-6210, WI
Timeless Touches, 623-362-8285, AZ
Tombow, 678-442-9224, GA
Toybox, 707-431-1400, CA
Tsukineko, 800-769-6633, WA
Two Peas in a Bucket, 608-827-0852, WI
US ArtQuest, 517-522-6225, MI
Walnut Hollow, 608-935-2341, WI
Westrim, 800-727-2727, CA
Wordsworth, 719-282-3495, CO
Z Barten, 800-266-3388, CA
Zettiology, www.zettiology.com, WA
Zig Markers, 800-524-1349, NJ

MANY THANKS to my friends for their cheerful help and wonderful ideas!
Kathy McMillan • Jen Tennyson
Patty Williams • Marti Wyble
Janet Long • Krystal Lewis
David & Donna Thomason

Renée Plains

Renée designed the elegant series of coordinated Legacy papers for DESIGN ORIGINALS. She loves the vintage colors of these papers to showcase the photos on her scrapbook pages. The TeaDye stained edges of the papers give them a rustic look that makes them especially appealing on frames and journals.

Renée enjoys working with fibers, papers, rubber stamps and vintage treasures to create artwork.

Renée is a quilt and doll designer. She publishes LIBERTY STAR patterns in Scottsdale, AZ. She teaches workshops around the country.

Tim Holtz

Tim is the Senior Educator and Designer for Ranger Industries. He teaches a variety of workshops and demonstrates at national conventions. Tim is never at a loss for creativity and enthusiasm. "Creativity is an endless journey where we should always take the scenic route."

Shannon Smith

In addition to operating her own invitations and cards business YOU'RE INVITED TOO, Shannon enjoys scrapbooking. She designs pages and cards for DESIGN ORIGINALS, BETTER HOMES AND GARDENS scrapbook magazine and for SCRAPBOOKS, ETC:

Delores Frantz

Delores is a talented craft designer. She has worked with scout groups for years, specializing in organized craft projects. Delores is often a guest, on television and has written numerous craft books.

Carol Winge

Carol lives with ... band Vern, and da ... ter, Ashley. She is ... instructor at MEM ... LANE in Gilbert, ... with current classe ... scrapbooking and book arts. Ca ... work has appeared on the cove ... LEGACY MAGAZINE and in CRE ... KEEPSAKES, with two Hall of F ... Honorable Mention awards.

Susan Keute

Susan lives with ... husband Greg and ... dren Elizabeth ... Thomas. She tea ... creative classes at ... SCRAPBOOK BARN ... Gilbert, AZ. Susan l ... having the opportunity to meet ... know others who are equally pas ... ate about cherishing family and so ... booking.

Shelley Pett

Shelley is manage ... and teacher at S ... SCRAPPIN & STAMPI ... Scarborough, Mo ... Shelley is a certifie ... Instructor. She and ... husband Joe have two teenage ... dren, Joey and Chrissy. "Thank yo ... all my loyal scrapbook friends for ... support and encouragement."

Laura Grego

Laura is owner of ... SCRAPBOOK PAGE in ... Worth, Texas. She ... native Texan wi ... degree from Ab ... Christian Univer ... Laura is mother to girls, Autumn ... Allie, and thanks her husband, C ... for his patience and love in helping ... achieve her goals and ambitions.

Create a small journal, a little album or a simple card.

ROLLABIND BOOK
by Renée Plains

MATERIALS: *Design Originals Legacy Papers* (#0480 Green floral, #0478 Green linen) • Cardstock • Small photo • Star nailhead • Rubber stamps (*Zettiology* label stamp; *Rubbermoon* 'xoxo' stamp; *Limited Edition* #8531H script) • Rollabind (Punch, small antique silver discs) • Adhesive

INSTRUCTIONS: Cut 5$^{1}/_{2}$" squares from cardstock and floral paper. Glue paper to cardstock • Cut a 3" square from cardstock and linen paper. Glue paper to cardstock and round corners. Stamp script stamp on square. Draw a line around the edge of square. Glue picture to square. Set nailhead above picture. Glue to cover • Stamp a small label on linen paper. Stamp 'xoxo' in label. Glue under picture on cover • Cut text weight paper into 5$^{1}/_{2}$" squares for the inside pages • Punch binding holes with a Rollabind hole punch along one side edge of cover and inside pages. Bind with Rollabind discs.

7 gypsies is a wonderful source for unusual accents and embellishments that look fabulous combined with *Legacy* papers from *Design Originals*. The colors and vintage look blend beautifully!
www.7gypsies.com

Legacy Papers
Design Originals,
2425 Cullen Street
Ft Worth, TX 76107
800-877-7820
www.d-originals.com
Embellishments & Charms
7 gypsies,
1275 E. Baseline Rd. #104
Gilbert, AZ 85233
480-325-3358
www.7gypsies.com